Hope in the Holler

Hope in the Holler

A Womanist Theology

A. Elaine Brown Crawford

Westminster John Knox Press
LOUISVILLE • LONDON

Scripture quotations from the New Revised Standard Version of the Bible are copyright © 1989 by the Division of Christian Education of the National Council of the Churches of Christ in the U.S.A. and are used by permission.

Excerpt from *Incidents in the Life of a Slave Girl* by Harriet Jacobs, © 1988 Oxford University Press. Reprinted by permission.

Book design by Sharon Adams
Cover design by Eric Walljasper, Minneapolis, MN
Cover photograph courtesy of Ron Krisel/Getty Images

First edition
Published by Westminster John Knox Press
Louisville, Kentucky

This book is printed on acid-free paper that meets the American National Standards Institute Z39.48 standard. ∞

PRINTED IN THE UNITED STATES OF AMERICA

02 03 04 05 06 07 08 09 10 11 — 10 9 8 7 6 5 4 3 2 1

Library of Congress Cataloging-in-Publication Data

Crawford, A. Elaine Brown (Anna Elaine Brown), 1947–
    Hope in the holler : a womanist theology / A. Elaine Brown Crawford.— 1st ed.
        p. cm.
    Includes bibliographical references.
    ISBN 0-664-22254-4 (pbk. : alk. paper)
        1. African American women—Religious life. 2. Womanist theology. I. Title.

BR563.N4 C72 2002
230'.082—dc21   2002071345

In memory of my sister, Doris J. Brown,
who died in the midst of her Holler

To my mother, Margaret J. Brown,
who "hopes" me through all my Hollers

Contents

Acknowledgments

*T*hough my name graces this book, several people contributed to its completion in very significant ways. This work is a labor of love, and as the nature of "labor" tends to be, it was at times a painful, arduous journey. Yet I rejoice in what has been birthed. I want to thank my mentor, colleague, and friend, Jacquelyn Grant, for her example of academic excellence, rigor, and commitment to the work. Her untiring efforts in my development as a scholar and a professional have been tremendously appreciated. My research year at the Interdenominational Theological Center in the Office of Black Women in Church and Society transformed my scholarship. Thank you, Jackie, for serving on my dissertation committee and taking time out of your unbelievable schedule to read this manuscript.

I am deeply indebted to Carey Newman, Julie Tonini, and Westminster John Knox Press for affirming my work and facilitating its publication. Carey, thank you for reading and rereading and for the confidence you evidenced in my scholarship.

Thank you to Katie Cannon, who helped me reclaim my voice. During my graduate studies, the weekly trips to Philadelphia to work with Katie were indeed life giving as well as life changing. I learned to breathe again. Thank you to Allison Gise Johnson, who provided a bed and meals for me on a weekly basis so that I could sit at the feet of the Jesus and genius of Katie Cannon.

I am deeply indebted to Dawn DeVries, Doug Ottati, and Donald Dawe for their direction, devotion, and faith in this project. Their academic rigor and demand of academic excellence helped shape my development as a theologian. My graduate studies and work at Union-PSCE provided me with a solid theological undergirding and excellent preparation for work in the academy and the church. Their work on my dissertation committee was challenging and at the same time affirming.

Thank you to John Kenny of the School of Theology at Virginia Union (STVU), whose passion and dedication to theology, and its liberative relevance for the black church, infected me as a seminary student at STVU.

I am grateful to many friends who encouraged and supported me through seminary and graduate work. Thanks to Nancy Long, whose friendship and emotional support helped me traverse the emotional roller-coaster ride of graduate work and life. Thanks to "D" for your friendship along the way. My prayer group in Richmond sustained me spiritually and prayed for me without ceasing. Those prayers held my arms up when I grew weary. I am grateful to all of my unnamed companions who took the time to listen to my rantings about hope and helped me think through the project. Thank you to the pastors and churches who embraced and supported my development and education with your prayers, money, and ministry opportunities. Specifically, I am grateful to The First Institutional Baptist Church, Phoenix, Arizona, where Dr. Warren H. Stewart Sr. is pastor; Dr. Kirkland Walton and the St. Peter Baptist Church of Richmond, Virginia; and the Reverend McCallister Hollins and the Ben Hill United Methodist Church family, Atlanta, Georgia.

I would also like to express to my family how much your support, sacrifice, and love sustained me in the midnight hours. Thank you to my adult children, Kim, Shari, and Ron, who believe that "Mom can do anything she sets her mind to." Your faithfulness blesses my life and helps make my work live. Thank you to my mom, who entered seminary at age sixty-two and inspired me to answer the call upon my life and enter seminary. Thank you to my brothers and sister—Billy, George, Stephen, Mark, Dale, and Alicia—for your support.

Though I am chronologically older than most of the first-generation womanist scholars, I thank them for preparing the way for the second generation. It is because of them that we have dialogue partners whose work and scholarship challenge us to do critical inquiry that is fresh, relevant, and usable. I thank them for carving out the creative space for womanist engagement across the disciplines.

Finally, I am grateful to God, who woke me from the midst of a deep sleep after a tear-filled night and told me that "there is Hope in the Holler."

Introduction: A Peculiar Hope

*H*ope is a perennial theme in theological discourse and has been explored and discussed in almost every age. The twentieth century witnessed a renewed and focused attention on this concept. In twentieth-century theological discourse, hope has been explored most fully in the work of Jürgen Moltmann and several critical responses to his work. Moltmann propelled the theology of hope to the forefront of theological debate in 1964 with his seminal work, *Theology of Hope: The Ground and Implications of Christian Eschatology*.[1]

This revitalized attention to the theme of hope is pertinent for the emerging womanist[2] theology, because hope has played a pivotal role in enabling African American women to overcome a legacy of abuse in the church and in society. African American women have been the "permissible victims"[3] of American society. They were the persons who could be victimized with little or no repercussions. African American women's bodies have been abused physically and sexually. Their existence has been scarred by the brutality and sexual exploitation of the middle passage and chattel slavery, as well as by the pervasive institutional and social forms of race, class, and gender oppression that persist to this day.

---

1. Jürgen Moltmann, *Theology of Hope: The Ground and Implications of Christian Eschatology* (New York: Harper & Row, 1967).

2. The term *womanist* was coined by Alice Walker in her work *In Search of Our Mothers' Garden: Womanist Prose* (San Diego: Harcourt Brace Jovanovich, 1983), xi–xii. The term is derived from the word *womanish* and refers to African American women as "courageous, audacious, concerned about family, community and relationship with God." Walker calls the womanist "a black feminist, a feminist of color." Womanists are concerned about the multidimensional oppression (minimally race, class, and gender) of African American women and women of color in general.

3. Frances Woods uses this term to designate groups or individuals that can be oppressed without consequences. The least permissible victim is the heterosexual, white, wealthy male. Woods, "Take My Yoke Upon You," in *A Troubling in My Soul: Womanist Perspectives on Evil and Suffering*, ed. Emilie M. Townes (Maryknoll, N.Y.: Orbis Books, 1993), 39–41, 46, n. 3.

African American women have lived in the echoes of their own Holler. The Holler is the primal cry of pain, abuse, violence, separation. It is a soul-piercing shrill of the African ancestors that demands the recognition and appreciation of their humanity. The Holler is the refusal to be silenced in a world that denied their very existence as women. The Holler is the renunciation of racialized and genderized violence perpetrated against them generation after generation. The Holler is a cry to God to "come see about me," one of your children.

Yet, African American women continue to endure, survive, and transform their oppressive existence. Hope is a foundational source of this audacity to survive the Holler, the inhumanities and injustices of life. This "unquenchable thirst for that which is not yet" is characterized as passion for life.[4] Hope, their passion for the possible in their lives,[5] has been voiced by African American women since slavery. This passion for the possible takes different forms in slavery (freedom, humanity), emancipation (voice), and contemporary narratives (autonomy and equality). Yet, in each era, the possible in their lives is understood as a this-worldly goal, intensely pursued. It is Hope in spite of and in the midst of the Holler.

The narratives of African American women who have suffered victimization through sexual abuse or physical violence reveal a distinctive discourse about hope: Hope is the theological construct that moves these women beyond endurance to survival and, ultimately, toward the transformation of oppressive circumstances. Hope is the bridge from oppression to liberation that facilitates full humanity and fosters an undaunted passion for life.

The character of hope across the generations and its function in the lives of African American women, as expressed in their own narratives, has not been thoroughly explored. Womanist discussions of hope, as well as theology more generally, will be enriched and expanded by extracting the meaning and function of hope from firsthand accounts in the narratives of black women.

While hope is not unique to abused African American women, hope does function distinctively in their lives due to the unique nature of their oppression. The peculiar quality of "black suffering" is characterized by three essential features. Black suffering is maldistributed (i.e., it is not spread evenly over humanity, since blacks suffer disproportionately); it is enormous in severity

---

4. Patricia Hunter, "Women's Power—Women's Passion," in *A Troubling in My Soul*, 192–93.

5. This understanding of hope is drawn from the work of Patricia Hunter and Søren Kierkegaard. Moltmann cites Kierkegaard as the source of the understanding of hope as a passion for the possible (*Theology of Hope*, 20). For Kierkegaard, hope is a form of possibility that is expressed through desiring or craving. The other form of possibility, he says, is despair. See Kierkegaard, *This Sickness Unto Death* (Princeton, N.J.: Princeton University Press, 1980), 37, 70–71; Søren Kierkegaard, *Christian Discourse* (London: Oxford University Press, 1939), 112–18.

(i.e., it is life-threatening, reducing life expectancy or one's ability to reach one's full potential); and it is non-catastrophic (i.e., it does not strike and leave quickly but is transgenerational, persisting over generations).[6] Moreover, African American women have suffered even greater victimization of their bodies because of gender injustices and inequities. Thus, in the midst of the Holler, African American women have had to formulate a distinctive hope to overcome their unique abuse.

Hope facilitates abused African American women's empowerment for life. While hope does have ultimate expression in the eschatological kingdom of God, its transformative power lies in its ability to transform the daily lives of African American women. Hope has been African American women's source of courage that makes living in the present possible and renders labor for a better tomorrow more than wishful thinking. Hope allows African American women to move from the role of victims, to empowered vessels—possessors and givers of life.[7]

In the chapters that follow, I identify and analyze the theology of hope operative in the lives of African American women. I do so by putting their vision of hope into conversation with current discussions of hope in womanist theology. Several womanist scholars have explored and extrapolated the injustices and inhumanities against African American women, but few have dug beneath the Holler to unearth the theology of hope that is the buried treasure in the stories. The Holler is the wellspring of hope. While my focus is the hope, the Holler is so loud that it reverberates in the texts we shall study. In what follows, we will listen for hope in selected narratives[8] of slave, emancipated, and finally contemporary abused African American women. We will explore the contours of hope in these three related but chronologically distinct sets of narratives. One must look to the narratives of slavery, because slavery provided the foundational expressions of hope in black women's lives. Out of the abuse and violence of slavery sprang a hope that has been passed on from generation to generation of black women. The narratives of emancipation demonstrate the thread of hope that connects slavery to contemporary narratives of abused women. From the voices of these narratives, I show how hope

---

6. William R. Jones, "Theodicy: The Controlling Category for Black Theology," in *Journal of Religious Thought* 30 (1973): 28–38.

7. The theme of black women being vessels, i.e., possessors and givers of life through the Holy Spirit, first emerges in the slave narrative of Old Elizabeth. She was a slave born in Maryland in 1766, who spent thirty years in bondage there. This theme continues in emancipated women's narratives. "Memoirs of Old Elizabeth, a Colored Woman," in *Six Women's Slave Narratives*, ed. Henry Louis Gates. Originally published in 1863 by Collins Printer (New York: Oxford University Press, 1988), 7–11.

8. *Narrative* refers to the life stories, firsthand accounts, written or dictated by the subject of the narrative.

functions in African American women's lives to enable them to endure, survive, and transform their own particular existential situation, both as individuals and as members of communities. I highlight the similarities and dissimilarities of hope across slavery, emancipation, and contemporary periods, as well as enlarge and enrich contemporary womanist visions of hope.

The method I will employ is *womanist textual analysis*.[9] The method is womanist in that it seeks to discern, from the selected narratives, the dynamics of multifocal oppression, minimally racism, classism, and sexism. Womanists analyze the relationship of multidimensional oppression and the abusive experiences of African American women, the Holler, as well as their expressions and embodiment of Hope.[10] Womanist analysis critiques structures, systems, and sociopolitical realities that foster domination/oppression of African American women particularly, the African community, and humanity in general. For womanists, the ever-present reality of multidimensional oppression is the *context* that has historically shaped, and continues to shape, the lives and work of African American women.[11]

The textual analysis is based on the understanding that part of the task of theology is clarifying or taking into account the context, content, and intent of sources.[12] The sociohistorical *context* out of which these narratives arise informs and influences their content. It influences what is written as well as how it is written. To fail to give attention to the context in which narratives are written invites misinterpretation of their contents. Context influences and provides a distinctive perspectival lens through which to interpret women's ways of negotiating the tapestry of relationships and structures that constitute their worlds.[13] Exploring context also reveals the varied activities and influences that permeate women's lives. Context is a "dynamic process through

---

9. I use this term to represent the merging of womanist critique with critical textual analysis.

10. I capitalize both Hope and Holler to emphasize the unique contours of African American women's expression of each. We will find from the narratives that the Hope is just as enormous as the Holler.

11. Womanist theologian Karen Baker-Fletcher notes:

The context out of which womanists construct theology and ethics is a complex context of struggle and celebration, evil and goodness, abuse and survival, bondage and liberation, illness and health, sorrow and hope. This is the context in which those who are Black [*sic*] and female in one body define what it means to be human in relation to God and work toward the survival, liberation, and wholeness of entire communities *male and female*. Karen Baker-Fletcher and Garth KASIMU Baker-Fletcher, *My Brother, My Sister: Womanist and Xodus God-Talk* (Maryknoll, N.Y.: Orbis Books, 1997), 7.

12. James Evans Jr. is one of many theologians who ascribes to this methodology. I have referenced his work because of his systematic treatment of African American theology and the kinship of his work to womanist methodology. James Evans, *We Have Been Believers: An African American Systematic Theology* (Minneapolis: Fortress Press, 1992), 3–9.

13. Personal Narrative Group, "Conditions Not of Her Own Making," in *Interpreting Women's Lives: Feminist Theory and Personal Narratives* (Bloomington: Indiana University Press, 1989), 19.

which the individual simultaneously shapes and is shaped by her environment."[14] One's context may be cultural, intellectual, spiritual, or social. Close attention to the context also exposes the threads of connectedness that interweave the lives of black women across the generations.

Analysis of the black women's experience, the *content* of their stories, reveals their "rugged determination"[15] for life that empowered them. The content of the narratives give voice to the religious sensibilities, theological themes, and distinctive expressions of hope in the lives of black women, as well as the particular forms of abuse and oppression they survived. Thus, the body of the narratives contains the content of faith and hope, as well as the experiences of oppression. The content of the stories shows the interweaving of the "canonical story" with African American women's stories. Black women's lives, their experiences and interpretations of those experiences, are thus a valid theological source. Katie Cannon argues that black women's lives, their bodies, and their experiences are the "canvas" upon which their stories and experiences of God have been written.[16] Cannon argues that one can turn to the literary traditions of black women, which include their narratives, to glean their struggles and theo-ethical consciousness. The black women's literary tradition, Cannon asserts, "is the best available repository for understanding the ethical [and theological] values Black women have created and cultivated in their ongoing participation in this society."[17] The narratives of black women document the "living space" black women have etched out for themselves as they negotiate the web of race, class, and gender oppression.

The *intent* of the narratives is an integral part of the selected women's stories. By *intent* of the narratives, I am referring to how hope functioned in these women's lives to move them beyond the Holler to actuate their personal and communal potential. Intent captures the theological and moral implications expressed in the narratives. Black women were empowered to take action by their faith in situations of oppression. They raised new questions and lived new responses. They preached a peculiar gospel about Christ, God, and the Holy Spirit in their everyday lives. Their hope was more than wishful thinking about what might be. Their passion for the possible in their lives directed the intent of their action. They struggled to actuate their hope for their own personal welfare as well as that of their family and community.

---

14. Ibid.

15. Evans, *We Have Been Believers*, 7.

16. See "Womanist Perspectival Discourse and Canon Formation," in *Katie's Canon: Womanism and the Soul of the Black Community* (New York: Continuum, 1995), 69–76, and the Introduction to Cannon's *Black Womanist Ethics* (Atlanta: Scholars Press, 1988), 2–6.

17. Cannon, *Black Womanist Ethics*, 7.

Context, content, and the theo-ethical implications of the selected narrative form concentric circles. Moving from the outer rim, context influences and shapes the inner circle, content. In the circle of content emerge the theo-ethical positions of each woman. As their theology and moral judgments mature and develop, the circle of influence reverses itself, so that their enlarged theo-ethical understandings then influence the content of their narratives. They understand themselves and their religious notions in new and enlarged ways. From the enlarged content we find these women affecting change in their lives, communities, and circumstances, their context.

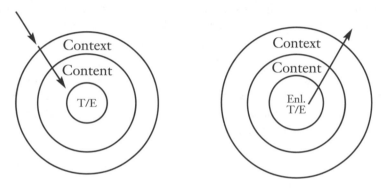

In the remaining pages, I do several things. First, chapter one accomplishes a number of goals. I introduce the problem of the lack of attention to the theology of hope in African American women's narratives through a discussion of hope in the work of Jacquelyn Grant, Delores Williams, and Karen Baker-Fletcher. I note that, while hope has been alluded to in the work of these womanist theologians, the voices of abused African American women have not been mined from their narratives to ascertain how hope was defined and how it functioned in their lives. Second, I introduce the context for the central chapters by exploring the sociohistorical framework of African American women's experiences of abuse. Third, I discuss the emergence of the African American literary tradition and the use of narratives as a vehicle by African American women. I finally turn to consider the influence of context on black women's narratives, discussing also the general criteria used for selecting narratives for this project, and how these narratives make clear the relationship between the Holler of abuse, hope, and religious expressions. In the central chapters (2, 3, and 4) I offer a womanist textual analysis of selected slave (chapter 2), emancipated (chapter 3), and contemporary (chapter 4) women's narratives to discern the implicit and explicit theological notions of hope voiced in these texts, and the function of hope in the women's daily lives. The central chapters examine the content and intent expressed in the selected narratives. The conclusion offers an analysis of the development of womanist notions of hope from slavery through today. The final chapter seeks to show the contributions and limits of contemporary womanist discussions of hope for abused African American women and to enlarge and enrich the discussion of hope from the voices of African American women's narratives. There is indeed Hope in the Holler.

Chapter 1

From Victim to Vessel:
Context of the Holler

*T*he voices of abused African American women from slavery and emancipation still echo in contemporary womanist expressions of hope. These voices provide the historical ground and theological roots of womanist hope. While the abuse of African American women's bodies certainly predates slavery, the discussion that follows is limited to the context in which firsthand accounts of black women's lives are available. As the sociohistorical context of black women changed, so did the function, expression, and embodiment of hope. While there are threads of hope that connect the centuries, the voices of black women are anything but monolithic. Thus, to arrive at a contemporary vision of hope for black women, we must explore the similarities and dissimilarities of each era—slavery, emancipation, and contemporary. The sociohistorical context of North America was and is so multitextured. Yet, a brief reference to the influence of slavery, emancipation, and the contemporary periods on the lives of black women seems appropriate before exploring the content of narratives in these periods.

Chattel slavery was a crucible of oppression of black women's bodies. The primal Holler of black foremothers is a resounding communal lament in the souls of African American women. The sexual and physical exploitation of black women's bodies that occurred in slavery influenced the treatment of black women during the emancipation and contemporary periods. Black slave women were objectified as property. They were viewed as animals, used as breeding women, surrogate wives, and manual laborers. Women worked in the fields and did the same type of labor as men. Childbirth and children did not exempt them from work. It was a sad reality that slave women were primarily full-time workers. Their roles as wife, mother, and homemaker were seen as secondary, incidental roles.[1] Though slavery eventually

---

1. Kenneth Stampp, *The Peculiar Institution: Slavery in the Antebellum South* (New York: Vintage Books, 1956), 343, as quoted in Emilie Townes, *Womanist Justice, Womanist Hope* (Atlanta: Scholars Press, 1993), 42.

ceased, the objectification of black women in society and in the church remained a tangible reality of the daily existence of black women. With emancipation came legal freedom, but the exploited economic condition of most black women required that most of them remain as servants on the very plantations on which they had been enslaved, or work as underpaid domestics or washerwomen. The sexual victimization of black women that was so common during slavery continued after emancipation, particularly for plantation and domestic workers. An elderly ex-slave summed up slavery and emancipation in an interview done in the 1930s:

> I can sit on the galley, where the sunlight shine bright, and sew a powerful fine seam when my grandchildren wants a special pretty dress for the school doings, but I ain't worth much for nothing else, I reckon.
>
> These old eyes seen powerful lots of tribulation in my time, and when I shuts them now I can see lots of little children just like my grandchildren, toting hoes bigger than they is, and they poor little black hands and legs bleeding where they was scratched by the bramble weeds, and where they got whippings cause they didn't get done all the work the overseer set out for them.
>
> I was one of them little slave girls my own self, and I never seen nothing but work and tribulation till I was a grown woman, just about. . . . It was the fourth of June in 1865 I begins to live. . . .
>
> I sho' thank de Lawd I got to see it.[2]

Work, tribulation, and "de Lawd" are central elements of slavery and postbellum life. These themes recur with great frequency in the narratives of slavery, emancipation, and the contemporary period. Work usually refers to burdensome and excessive physical labor on plantations and in homes, fields, churches, or organizations. Tribulation includes a vast array of "troubles," such as whippings, mutilation, sexual abuse, breaking up of families, various forms of physical abuse, lynching, unpaid or low-paying jobs, and dehumanizing acts perpetrated against one because of gender, race, or class. These troubles engendered the "Holler." "De Lawd" provided the hope in the Holler. "De Lawd" is frequently the source of overcoming the oppression unleashed upon black women. The narratives show a consistent reliance on God that engenders hope and aids black women to overcome the victimization of the sociohistorical context. And contemporary narratives will show that oppression of black women came not just from the dominant white culture, but, as recorded in black women's narratives, from within the black community and church as well.

---

2. Kate Rowe, ex-slave interview as quoted in James Mellon, ed., *Bullwhip Days: The Slaves Remember* (New York: Avon Books, 1988), 27–32.

The abuse of black women in all three eras is greatly influenced by the social myths projected onto black women that are prevalent in the various time frames. Slavery characterized black women as "Jezebels," hypersexual, amoral beasts, or as overweight, sexually docile women called "Mammies." Emancipation deepened the Jezebel and Mammy stereotypes of black women through newspapers and other media. Black women were also depicted as "Negro wenches," who led white and black men into moral degradation. By the early to mid-twentieth century, African American women were seen as hypersexual "bad black women." From the late twentieth century through today, "Sapphire," a dominating and emasculating black female, is the myth that has been used to define black women. These myths influence the treatment of black women in that they legitimize abuse. These social myths have influenced the content of black women's narratives that document their abuse and violation. Black women wrote to debunk dehumanizing stereotypes, to expose their abuse, and to claim their personhood and humanity through the telling of their own stories to empower others. Yet in spite of oppression, black women have been empowered by their faith and trust in the Lord to take action. Their narratives contain a theology of hope that empowered them to endure, survive, and even transform oppressive circumstances.

An analysis of the narratives of slave, emancipated, and contemporary black women reveals the contours of hope in the lives of abused African American women. The narratives give voice, from the perspective of African American women, to the theological source and function of hope in their lives. To broaden and deepen the doctrine of hope in theology, it is necessary to begin with contemporary womanist discussions of hope and only then bring them into conversation with the theology of hope found in the narratives of slave, emancipated, and contemporary black women. These narratives provide the sources that can be used to develop a prolegomenon to a contemporary womanist theology of hope.

Twentieth-Century Discussions of Hope

Womanist thought emerges at the intersection of black liberation theology and feminist theology. Remarkably, the concept of hope found in these movements, however, is insufficient: it does not accurately represent the function of hope in the lives of abused African American women. The limits of this work do not permit a thorough exploration of the literature in black liberation and feminist theology; however, a brief review of some of the discussions of hope in both movements underscores the need for the present study.

Black Liberation Theology

Twentieth-century black liberation theologians have had a variety of critical responses to the theological notion of hope, primarily in response to Moltmann's eschatological discussion of hope. For example, G. Clark Chapman Jr. discusses hope as an openness to the future that discerns God's involvement in humanity.[3] However, Chapman says that black theology finds Moltmann's understanding of the theology of hope "too oriented to the future and set in a context too alien to the black experience."[4] A theology about the future is possible for whites, Chapman asserts, who have a degree of security and status in the present. But for blacks facing day-to-day struggles for existence, a theology of the future is an impermissible luxury.[5]

J. Deotis Roberts agrees with Chapman's understanding of the future and its relevance to black theology. Roberts concludes:

> Instead of moving from the future to the present, we move from the present to the future—at least to begin. Only after we are aware of what God is doing in this world to make life more human for blacks may we speak of God's future breaking into our present and look forward to the new age.[6]

James Cone criticizes North American theologians for becoming excited with this "new" theology of hope. He says they have completely ignored the hope that has emerged over the last 350 years from the struggle of African Americans. Hope, as eschatology, must be realized in the here and now, says Cone, for hope to be relevant to black Christians.[7] For Cone, Christian eschatology has to be connected to the resurrection of Jesus. Cone asserts that Christ:

> . . . is the eschatological hope. He is the future of God who stands in judgement upon the world and forces us to give an account of the present. In view of his victory over evil and death, why must human beings suffer and die? Why do we behave as if the present were a fixed reality and not susceptible of radical change? As long as we look at the resurrection of Christ and the

---

3. G. Clark Chapman, "Black Theology and Theology of Hope: What Have They to Say to Each Other?" in *Black Theology: A Documentary History, 1966–1979* (Maryknoll, N.Y.: Orbis Books, 1979), 193–215.

4. Ibid., 197.

5. Ibid., 198.

6. J. Deotis Roberts, *Liberation and Reconciliation: A Black Theology* (Philadelphia: Westminster Press, 1971), 57.

7. James H. Cone, *God of the Oppressed* (New York: Seabury Press, 1988), 126–32.

expected "end," we cannot reconcile ourselves to the things of the present that contradict his presence. It is this eschatological emphasis that black theology affirms.[8]

Hope, for Cone, must be an agent for transforming the oppressed community into a liberated community.

Major Jones discusses black theology and the church's role in infusing Christian hope in its members and in the world. Jones states that a black theology of hope must be relevant outside of the academy and develop "a new correlation between the eschatological origins of Christian faith and present revolutionary forces that seek to build a new and better future for the black man."[9] Jones argues that too much of black theology is devoid of hope and has focused primarily on the despair of life. He articulates hope as the intersection between faith and social-political action that fosters betterment for African Americans through nonviolence as a method of revolution. For Jones, this co-relational relationship between eschatology and the human condition requires an anthropology of hope that is oriented to the future of the black man. To provide a theology that speaks cogently and realistically to oppressed peoples whose lives have been dehumanized by words and actions perpetrated by the dominant culture, and whose hopes have been consistently frustrated, requires, for Jones, a new and fresh message of hope for the future.[10] Thus, black liberation theology has not articulated its hope; rather, it has responded to other notions of hope.

Black theology's understanding of hope, as articulated by Chapman, Roberts, Cone, and Jones, has been limited in two ways. First, it has primarily responded to Moltmann's notion of hope as its starting point, but second and even more important, its critique has primarily been based on the experience of racism. Victor Anderson challenges black theology to move beyond racial analysis as the primary focus of critique. He calls this limited discourse "ontological blackness" and says it connotes "categorical, essentialist, and representational languages depicting black life and experience."[11] Discussions of hope from the feminist perspective have a similar single-vision analysis.

---

8. James H. Cone, *A Black Theology of Liberation: Twentieth Anniversary Edition* (Maryknoll, N.Y.: Orbis Books, 1993), 140.

9. Major Jones, *Black Awareness: A Theology of Hope* (Nashville: Abingdon Press, 1971), 12.

10. Ibid., 13.

11. Victor Anderson, *Beyond Ontological Blackness: An Essay on African American Religious and Cultural Criticism* (New York: Continuum, 1995), 11.

Feminist Theology

Feminist notions of hope are equally limited in their applicability to the experiences of African American women. Hope is discussed in feminist theology from the perspective of white women's experience—primarily their experience of sexism. Elizabeth Johnson understands hope as an *individual* (not *communal*, like black women) virtue. In her work on feminist theology as critical discourse about God, Johnson discusses hope as conversion rather than eschatology. She understands hope, that is, the conversion experience, for women as turning away from negating self, from acceptance of sexism, to empowering self. Foundational to a feminist understanding of conversion is a "protest against suffering caused by sexism and a turning to the flourishing of women in all their concrete femaleness."[12] For Johnson, conversion experience involves contrast and conversion. Contrast is inherent between the suffering of sexism and the humanity of women, while confirmation points to the agency and power of women. Both contrast and confirmation are mediated by the same Christian tradition, argues Johnson. Feminist theology must deconstruct and reconstruct understandings of hope as conversion, and articulate a theological paradigm shift that denotes the transformative possibilities for women's lives.

Speech about God, theology, becomes a primary source of constructing women's lives and hope. However, theological speech is often speech about God that is constructed in exclusively patriarchal terms. Such speech "debilitates women's sense of dignity, power, and self-esteem."[13] Johnson notes that "exclusively patriarchal imagery for the divine functions as a tool of symbolic violence against the full self-identity of female persons, blocking their identity as images of God and curtailing their access to divine power."[14] Conversion experience is the fundamental character of hope, for Johnson, and is actualized by Sophia-Spirit shaping the world.

Rosemary Radford Ruether explores three patterns of hope. She relates feminism and hope to eschatology in nature religions (ancient Near Eastern), historical religions (Hebraic), and eschatological religions (Persian, Hellenistic-Constantine). The nature religions, Ruether asserts, espoused the renewal of nature as a key to a hope for the renewal of life. Historical hope locates the ultimate achievement of humanity in the final era of world history. It offers no immediate answer to the suffering and death of the present. Ruether argues

---

12. Elizabeth Johnson, *She Who Is: The Mystery of God in Feminist Theological Discourse* (New York: Crossroad, 1992), 29, 61–65, 73, 137–39, 169.

13. Ibid., 38.

14. Ibid.

that eschatological religions sever hope from history.[15] The tendency of modern theology, says Ruether, to label all these relations "eschatological" is misleading and confusing. For Ruether, the term *eschatology* should be reserved to denote "a view that believes in the possibility of human transcendence of mortality."[16]

Ruether asserts that Christian eschatology is ambiguous toward women and has come under severe critique by feminist theology. Biblical religions and modern revolutionary movements have been based on a linear view of history in which the final millennium ushers in the overcoming of evil and the reign of goodness. This endless flight into the future, argues Ruether, "idolizes change and fails to respect the relational patterns of our bodies as ground of holy being."[17] Ruether suggests a different model of hope. She develops hope under the rubric of "historical" and "personal eschatology." *Historical eschatology*, for Ruether, must involve conversion, or *metanoia*. She understands conversion to mean that the basic ingredients for a just and livable society are rooted in the balance between nature and the acceptance of human finitude. This balance is the Shalom of God/ess that allows "conversion to the earth and to each other, rather than the flight into the unrealizable future."[18] She also asserts that *personal eschatology* provides the answers to the questions of suffering in this life. The appropriate response to these questions, for Ruether, is an agnosticism. We cannot know about that which has not been revealed to us as humans, nor can we project our wishes upon our future. What is known to humanity is that death is the cessation of life, and hope, and that our existence "dissolves back into the cosmic matrix of matter/energy."[19] Personal eschatology, she asserts, will lead to beloved communities of mutuality and support based on human beings accepting responsibility for the generations to come.

Both of these feminist treatments of hope are of limited value for womanists. Johnson discusses hope from the perspective of a white, middle-class woman whose point of departure for theological discussions is sexism. Her understanding of hope does not capture the multidimensional oppression that African American women have endured and survived. Ruether's discussion of hope is limited because she views hope as a purely human construct. Her historical and personal eschatology contradict the notion of "God with us in

---

15. Rosemary Ruether, *Sexism and God-Talk: Toward a Feminist Theology* (Boston: Beacon Press, 1983), 237–45.
16. Ibid., 240.
17. Ibid., 254.
18. Ibid., 255–56.
19. Ibid., 257.

the time of struggle" that pervades African American women's narratives. Though Ruether calls for a "personal eschatology," black women's narratives show that, historically, relationships between black and white women often mirror the patriarchal/domination model of the larger society. Thus, communities of mutuality and support are not possible as long as racism, classism, and white women's "privilege of patriarchy"[20] continue to exist.

Both black liberation theology and feminist theology have offered critiques that are one-dimensional. Black theology was primarily concerned with racism, while feminist theology focused on sexism. For black women, oppression is multidimensional. One-dimensional analysis does not elucidate the context of oppression or the emergence of hope for black women.

Womanist Theology

This discussion leads us to two salient questions. What then is hope to African American women? How does hope function in their lives in light of the multidimensional oppression they experience on a daily basis, and what is the source or ground of their hope? I maintain that we have not sought the answers to these questions where we should: from the mouths of black women. We must reconsider hope in African American women's experience and voices. While hope has been discussed widely in twentieth-century theology, even womanist notions of hope do not adequately elucidate the meaning and function of hope in the voice of abused African American women.

Womanist theologians have consistently attributed the survival of African American women to their "strength" or courage in adversity and interpret this strength as hope. According to Delores Williams, womanist hope involves Christians working together to alleviate the sin of defilement and devaluation that threatens the lives and spirits of African American women. Williams, like black liberation theologians, explores hope through a dialogue with biblical narratives. She argues that the Genesis narratives about Hagar provide a more appropriate biblical foundation for womanist hope than the Exodus passages of the Israelites' liberation, traditionally used by black liberation theologians. Hagar reveals the hope and struggle with which African American women have worked through issues of survival, surrogacy, motherhood, rape, homelessness, and economic and sexual

---

20. Womanist theologian Delores Williams uses this phrase to discuss the view that patriarchy has a positive side for white women, by virtue of their skin color, that is not extended to black women and their children. See Williams, "A Womanist Perspective on Sin," in *A Troubling in My Soul: Womanist Perspectives on Evil and Suffering*, ed. Emilie Townes (Maryknoll, N.Y.: Orbis Books, 1993), 149, n. 45.

oppression.[21] Williams writes very graphically about the abuse of black women's bodies and connects this abuse to the theological implications of glorifying the death of Jesus on the cross. For Williams, Jesus was the ultimate surrogate, and to glorify the cross is tantamount to condoning the bloody, brutal abuse of Christ's body. Further, she argues, to accept the cross as salvific is to sacralize abuse. Black women's hope is, in part, predicated upon Christian symbols that affirm life for all humanity rather than glorifying abuse.

Jacquelyn Grant talks about the black[22] woman's active hope in Jesus, particularly in abusive situations. She elucidates womanist hope from the christological perspective by discussing Jesus as the Divine co-sufferer, who empowers black women in situations of oppression. Grant says that the resurrected Jesus inspires womanist hope and empowers the struggle for resurrected, liberated existence.[23] She compares black and white women's experience during and after slavery, yet she does not attend, to a great extent, to the voices of black women's hope in their narratives in these eras. Grant references several slave narratives that clearly demonstrate the interplay of racism and sexism[24] and the sexual exploitation of black women's bodies. One function that black women served for white men, she notes, was to "bear the brunt of their sexual exploitation."[25] Grant also attends to the image of blacks during the antebellum and postbellum periods. She notes that white people's image of black women (and men) influenced their treatment. She does go to the voices of slaves to extract their understanding of Jesus. The

---

21. Delores Williams, *Sisters in the Wilderness: The Challenges of Womanist God-Talk* (Maryknoll, N.Y.: Orbis Books, 1993), 2–8, 15–33; Williams, "Sin, Nature, and Black Women's Bodies," in *Ecofeminism and the Sacred*, ed. C. Adams (New York: Continuum, 1993); Williams, "A Womanist Perspective on Sin," in *A Troubling in my Soul*, 130–47, 149 n. 45; Williams, "Women's Oppression and Lifelong Politics in Black Women's Religious Narratives," in *Journal of Feminist Studies in Religion* 1 (fall 1985): 59–71; Williams, "Vision, Inner Voices, Apparitions, and Defiance in Nineteenth-Century Black Women's Narratives," in *Women's Studies Quarterly* 21 (spring/summer 1993): 81–89.

22. I use *black*, rather than *African American*, to follow the authors' wording. I see the two terms as interchangeable and use them within their appropriate historical frames.

23. Jacquelyn Grant, *White Women's Christ and Black Women's Jesus: Feminist Christology and Womanist Response* (Atlanta: Scholars Press, 1989), 209–18; Jacquelyn Grant, "Come to My Help, Lord, for I'm in Trouble: Womanist Jesus and the Mutual Struggle for Liberation," in *Reconstructing the Christ Symbol*, ed. M. Stevens (New York: Friendship Press, 1989); Jacquelyn Grant, "A Refusal to Be Silenced: Reflections on Sojourner Truth," *Sojourners* 15 (1986): 23–25; Jacquelyn Grant, "Womanist Theology: Black Women's Experience as a Source for Doing Theology, with Special Reference to Christology," in *Journal of the Interdenominational Theological Center* 13 (spring 1986): 195–212.

24. Grant makes several references to narratives and biographies of slave women who suffered the abuses of slavery. She sets this discussion in the context of white-black women's relationship and white women's privilege and protection of patriarchy. See Grant, *White Women's Christ and Black Women's Jesus*, 223–24, n. 3.

25. Ibid., n. 4.

hope of black women, she argues, is christological. Though the life and death of Jesus are significant for her, "it is the resurrected Black Christ that signifies this hope (liberation from oppression)."[26] The resurrection signifies that oppression is merely the context in which hope is experienced. Williams has done some work with the slave narratives and discusses black women's oppression across the generations. Yet, like Grant, she has not explored the function of hope in their narratives. Hope as a passion for the possible in life that is transgenerational in nature has been alluded to but not expounded upon in womanist discourse.

Karen Baker-Fletcher takes a more traditional Western approach to the discussion of hope. She defines hope in terms of Western theological categories as eschatological. Eschatology, for Baker-Fletcher, includes "the transformation of society and all creation with it from what it is to what it ought to be according to God's vision for the world."[27] Her discussion of hope centers on the kingdom of God which is at hand. She connects this with the biblical passage in Psalm 27 that says, regardless of the presence of evildoers in the world, the faithful are empowered by God to transform personal and social oppression. Baker-Fletcher references the courage and audacity of black women like Sojourner Truth, Harriet Tubman, and women in the Black Women's Club movement as examples of womanist hope. Though she references hope as eschatological, she makes a point to emphasize that black women's hope is the day-to-day business of living now, not just in the "end times." Yet, like Williams and Grant, Baker-Fletcher does not explore the voices of abused black women for their understanding of hope.

The discussions by Williams, Grant, and Baker-Fletcher are helpful, but limited. Womanist theologians have not sufficiently explored expressions of hope from the voices of victimized African American women. Their discussions are even more limited in their ability to shed light on the transgenerational character of hope in the lives of African American women from slavery to today. To glean black women's understanding of hope, to discuss how it functioned in their lives, and to uncover the source of that hope, we must listen to *their voices*.

To mine all of the narratives of black women in order to glean their understanding of hope would be a life's work of theological archaeology. The discussion of hope for womanist theology is too important to wait for the results of such extensive excavation. This research is important for womanist the-

---

26. Ibid., 216.
27. Karen Baker-Fletcher and Garth KASIMU Baker-Fletcher, *My Brother, My Sister: Womanist and Xodus God-Talk* (Maryknoll, N.Y.: Orbis Books, 1997), 285.

ology because the drumbeat of hope that empowers the community has been paled in the clamor of the Holler. Hope has played a pivotal role in the lives and religious development of African American women, yet their voices have not been fully heard. Thus, I have adopted an "interim strategy" by which I have selected narratives from each period to formulate some introductory statements and assessments for a contemporary womanist theology of hope.

The selection of appropriate narratives for this project has been guided by several criteria. I will introduce and cite specific selected narratives in their respective chapters. Here I set forth some general statements regarding the criteria for selecting the narratives used. (1) All of the narratives are firsthand accounts by African American women. Part of what is lacking in womanist discussions of hope is sufficient attention to the voices of African American women. (2) Each narrative relates the experience of abuse and/or the woman's expression of hope. This elucidates the dialectic interaction between hope and the Holler. (3) The narratives relate the experiences of abuse and notions of hope to the concepts of God, self, or community. (4) The narratives include the voices of various socioeconomic groups because the dialectic between abuse and hope is not limited to a particular group of African American women, but spans the lives of black women in various socioeconomic groups. (5) Slave narratives were selected from narratives written or dictated by slave women during de jure slavery because the structure and rhetorical strategies of narratives altered drastically once de jure slavery, in which they were written and read, ceased.[28] It was impossible for a free person to see things from the same perspective as an enslaved person.[29] (6) Narratives of emancipated women fall between 1866 and the 1950s.[30] I use the term *emancipation*

---

28. Charles Davis and Henry Louis Gates, eds., *The Slave's Narrative* (New York: Oxford University Press, 1985), xii–xiii, 319–27.

29. Paraphrased from a quote of Frederick Douglass, *My Bondage and My Freedom* (New York: 1855): 339, as cited in Davis and Gates, *The Slave's Narrative*, 94.

30. I have drawn emancipated women's narratives primarily from the forty-one-volume, indexed collection of ex-slave interviews edited by George Rawick, *The American Slave: A Composite Autobiography* (Westport, Conn.: Greenwood Press, 1972). The series is formally known as the Federal Writer's Project Slave Narratives of the Work Progress Administration (WPA) and is referred to as the WPA Slave Narratives. These narratives are called "folk" narratives by Will Coleman because they are interviews of "average" black folk who did not publish their stories and would probably never have published their views of slavery without the WPA interviews. I have also drawn from classic "slave" narratives. These are narratives written with the abolitionist intent of exposing the horrors of slavery. The slave narratives used here were published by the narrator or a hired publisher at least ten years after the end of de jure slavery, and are, according to Davis's definition, cited in criterion number 5, ex-slave narratives. These narratives tend to be short, two-to-three-page expressions. While both folk and classic narratives reflect on life as a slave, they also illumine the hope of oppressed African American women.

narratives broadly to include those narratives written after slavery and before the contemporary period. (7) Contemporary women's narratives are those published from the 1960s through the present.[31] These periods, emancipation and the contemporary era, are watersheds marked by the rise of modernity, the civil rights movement, the black power movement, and a resurgence of women's liberation movements. Yet, even when guided by these seven criteria, there are more narratives than I can attend to in this study.

Having set out the criteria for selecting narratives to explore, we must now turn to religious responses to suffering and the foundational questions that prompt this work.

Religious Responses to Evil and Suffering

In theological terms, black women's questions about the justice of God in the midst of suffering were inextricable from their understandings of hope.[32] While evil and suffering are not identical, they are inseparable. Questions of suffering and evil confront all of humanity. The experiences of slavery, emancipation, and life in the contemporary period each contain their own form of moral evil[33] expressed through individual acts as well as through socially constructed acts of evil. Socially constructed evil devalues, dehumanizes, and marginalizes particular groups of peoples. Its pattern of relationships is hierarchical, subordinating the dignity of one group to another. Such dehumanization is often the source of existential and physical suffering, including death.

Suffering is a by-product of evil. Yet, religious responses to suffering can be both positive and negative, and can function in several ways. First, as Stephen Vicchio argues, religious responses to suffering have an existential function. They can, he asserts, attempt to provide a context that integrates the

---

31. Contemporary narratives of abused black women include: Kay Mills, *This Little Light of Mine: The Life of Fannie Lou Hamer* (New York: Plume Books, 1993); Maya Angelou, *I Know Why the Caged Bird Sings* (New York: Random House, 1970); Andrea R. Canaan, "I Call Up Names Facing Childhood Sexual Abuse," in *The Black Women's Health Book: Speaking for Ourselves*, ed. Evelyn C. White (Seattle: Seal Press, 1990), 78–81; Linda Hollies, "A Daughter Survives Incest: A Retrospective Analysis," in *The Black Women's Health Book*, 82–91; Evelyn White, "Love Don't Always Make It Right: Black Women and Domestic Violence," in *The Black Women's Health Book*, 92–97.

32. The classical theological question of evil centers around the problem of reconciling the historical presence of evil and the belief that God is the all-good, all-powerful Creator of the universe.

33. The evil that results from human choice and acts of free will is what is generally understood as *moral* evil. The evil that occurs as a result of hurricanes, flood, earthquakes, etc. is referred to as *natural* evil.

existence of evil into the lived reality of being human.[34] This context integrates both moral and natural evil into the larger picture of corporeality. It enables one to speak to what Tillich calls the "boundary situations" of life—those situations in which our ability to say yes to life is threatened.

Religious responses to suffering can also make suffering more bearable. Clifford Geertz noted that "[t]he problem of suffering is, paradoxically, not how to avoid suffering, but how to make physical pain, personal loss, and worldly defeat, or the helpless contemplation of others' agony something bearable, supportable, as we say, sufferable."[35] Religious responses to suffering also function to provide a coherent, intellectual means of helping sufferers give meaning to their experience of suffering. For the theologian as well as the peasant, theodicies grapple with the questions of suffering and seek "to demonstrate that the suffering of the innocent does not negate the conception of a God both all good and all powerful."[36] The making of meaning does not provide false hope, happiness, or a "promise of redemption at all except the redeeming assurance of meaning itself."[37] Peter Berger notes the individual and the social function of meaning. Individuals desire relief from suffering, exploitation, oppression, and torment but the "desire to know why these manifestations have come in the first place"[38] is equally strong. The providing of meaning, he asserts, serves a very important function in the lives of individual sufferers even if happiness, in this life or the world to come, is not the promised outcome of suffering.

Religious responses to suffering can also have a negative social function. They can produce the negative response of legitimating the status quo. They explain "the socially prevailing inequalities of power and privilege."[39] They legitimate the powerful and the powerless, the privileged and the deprived. The slave master's religion, the "religion of America," served such a legitimizing function. It answered the questions of theodicy by justifying the maintenance of slavery and the dehumanization of black people. It sanctioned treating them as less than humans created in the image of God.

---

34. Stephen J. Vicchio, *Voice from the Whirlwind: The Problem of Evil and the Modern World* (Westminster, Md.: Christian Classics, 1989), 5.

35. Clifford Geertz, *The Interpretation of Culture* (New York: Basic Books, 1973), 104.

36. Peter Berger, *The Sacred Canopy: Elements of a Sociological Theory of Religion* (Garden City, N.Y.: Doubleday & Co., Inc., 1967), 53. In this text, Berger develops an elaborate typology for differentiating between various types of theodicy making and responses to suffering.

37. Ibid., 58.

38. Ibid.

39. Ibid., 59.

Anthony Pinn suggests that for black people, suffering leads one to the question "Why, Lord?" He proposes a humanistic rather than a theistic approach to questions of evil and suffering.[40] For Pinn, "human liberation is more important than the maintenance of any religious symbol, sign, canon, or icon."[41] Redemptive suffering, Pinn asserts, is never a part of the quest for liberation. The two, suffering and redemption, are diametrically opposed to each other; one nullifies the other. William R. Jones suggests that, not only is suffering never redemptive, but if an all-powerful God allowed the oppression and suffering of black people, then God must be a white racist.[42]

In light of this discussion one must ask several questions regarding black women's responses to evil and suffering. Did their suffering negate their concept of an all-powerful God? Did the Christian religion and the Bible legitimize their suffering? How do black women understand the nature of a God who allows the suffering of black human beings? Does hope come in the midst of, or in spite of, oppression or both? What is hope for black women and how does it function in their lives? These questions can best be answered from the voices and experiences recorded in their narratives.

In chapter 2 we begin the womanist textual analysis of selected narratives written during de jure slavery. This analysis pays attention to the role of race, class, and gender oppression in specific sociohistorical context. It also attends to the myths that undergirded black women's oppression, influenced the content of black women's narratives, and empowered their embodied hope and resistance.

---

40. Pinn names himself a theologian although he believes that God does not exist. His rationale is that human suffering makes clear that an all-powerful, loving God is only a human projection. Humans inflict suffering upon other humans, and it is incumbent upon humans to work toward alleviating this suffering. See his discussion in Anthony B. Pinn, *Why, Lord? Suffering and Evil in Black Theology* (New York: Continuum, 1995).

41. Pinn, *Why, Lord?*, 11.

42. See William R. Jones, *Is God a White Racist? A Preamble to Black Theology* (Garden City, N.Y.: Anchor Press, 1978).

Chapter 2

Managing Secrets with Our Pen

*S*lavery was the genesis of the nascent expressions of the Holler and, ironically, the hope deposited in the narratives of black women. The theology of hope, born in slavery, was an active hope of resistance. The womanist textual analysis of slave narratives will show that slave women possessed a radical incarnational hope, given by God, and lived by enslaved humans. Hope, in the enslaved community, was expressed as a "passion for the possible" in this life.[1] The slave's hope was primarily a penultimate, this-worldly hope. Slaves were concerned about daily life on earth. The hope of slave women centered around their passion for the possible: freedom, humanity, voice, self-determination, and equality *in this world* as well as in the world to come. Their vision of what was to come in this world ignited their determination to survive and their courage to strive toward freedom. Such hope was more than an eschatological "end time" vision of possibilities. The eschaton functioned proleptically in their lives. "The transcendent future was also the present. The 'home over yonder' and the 'promised land' . . . were both an 'otherworldly' promise and a 'this worldly' hope for freedom."[2] This passion for the possible in their lives expressed by black women during slavery can be seen in their narratives, and it provides a foundational voice for a contemporary womanist theology of hope.

Three reasons make this study compelling and mandatory. First, the slave narratives cited in this chapter are the firsthand accounts of enslavement by

---

1. Hope as a passion for the possible is drawn from the Kierkegaardian notion of hope, as cited in Moltmann, *Theology of Hope: The Ground and Implications of Christian Eschatology* (New York: Harper & Row, 1967), 20. This passion takes different forms—freedom, humanity, voice, control of one's life, and equality—yet it is understood to have a this-worldly goal.
2. George Cummings, "The Slave Narrative as a Source of a Black Theological Discourse: The Spirit and Eschatology," in *Cut Loose Your Stammering Tongue: Black Theology in the Slave Narratives*, ed. Dwight Hopkins and George Cummings (Maryknoll, N.Y.: Orbis Books, 1991), 58.

black women.[3] Part of what is lacking in the discussion of hope is attention to the actual voices of abused African American women. The intent of this study is to capture the perspectival lens of the slave women whose voices have been virtually silenced in history. Exploring the narratives of slavery is foundational to discerning the cross-generational hope that interweaves the lives of black women. Second, these autobiographical accounts were written or dictated before 1866, during de jure slavery.[4] Of the 106 narratives written between 1760 and 1865 during de jure slavery, only 12 percent were written by women.[5] I have selected this time frame because the structure of the narratives changed with the end of de jure slavery. The abolitionist intent of the narratives was no longer a central theme once physical slavery ceased. Third, I have selected narratives that are representative of slave women's lives. I base this assumption on the fact that these narratives are accepted by historians and theologians as nonfictional, historical narratives of enslavement. Each of the women I write about was a victim of sexual or physical violence. I have narrowed my sources by looking at narratives that express physical or sexual violence because the racial violence of slavery is implicit in all the slave narratives, while the presence of physical or sexual violence is in many ways a uniquely female legacy under slavery. I have sought to ascertain from the voice of each woman the hope that sustained her in the midst of oppression.[6]

The distinctive character of black women's hope is the mirror image of black people's suffering. There is a particular quality of "black suffering" that is characterized by three essential features. Black suffering is: (1) maldistributed, not spread evenly over humanity, as blacks suffer disproportionately;

---

3. The authenticity of the Harriet Jacobs narrative as a first-person work has been a topic of discussion. The authenticity of the narrative, in my mind, has been established and substantiated by the work of Yellin (and other scholars) and the cache of Jacobs's letters. See Jean Fagan Yellin, "Text and Context of Harriet Jacobs's *Incidents in the Life of a Slave Girl: Written by Herself,*" in *The Slave's Narrative*, ed. Charles T. Davis and Henry Louis Gates Jr. (New York: Oxford University Press, 1985), 262–82. Also see n. 2, 278.

4. Other black theologians (including Will Coleman, Dwight Hopkins, and George Cummings) who have used the slave narratives as a theological source have focused primarily on the ex-slave interviews collected in the mid-1930s by the Federal Works Project. These interviews are known as WPA narratives. They are a rich source for understanding the life, experiences, and religious development of the black community. The WPA narratives number in the thousands. George Warwick collected and indexed the narratives by state and subject matter, and facilitated their use by scholars. I will consider a few of these narratives in my discussion of the period of emancipation.

5. Davis and Gates, *The Slave's Narrative*, 83.

6. I have eliminated narratives that are secondhand accounts of women's experiences, such as those written by men. I have avoided those narratives that have been determined by scholars to be fictional, that is, first-person accounts that mirror the atrocities of slavery, yet cannot be verified as accurate historical reports. I have avoided grouping all narratives written *about* slavery into the slave narrative genre, i.e., ex-slave interviews collected in the 1930s.

(2) enormous in severity, life-threatening, as it reduces life expectancy or one's ability to reach his or her full potential; and (3) non-catastrophic, that is, it does not strike quickly and leave, but is transgenerational.[7] Because of gender injustices, black women have suffered even greater victimization of their bodies. They are the distinctive within the distinctive. Black women have had to formulate *Hope* in a distinctive way to overcome this abuse: their hope is *maldistributed*, present in an inordinate number, to counter their rampant oppression; their hope is *enormous* in its ability to affirm humanity, proclaim their presence, and foster their ability to reach unrealized power, potential, and passion; and their hope is *transgenerational* and *non-catastrophic*; it functions as a spiritual bridge between oppression and liberation that interweaves the lives of black women across generations.

Specifically, this chapter analyzes the narratives of Mary Prince, Old Elizabeth, Sojourner Truth, and Harriet Jacobs. Through a close reading of their narratives, I seek to discern several elements from their life stories. First, I look for the specific impetus that led each woman to write her narrative. Next, I try to discern how this impetus for writing informs the expression of hope. Finally, I explore how each woman's religious understanding influenced her understanding of oppression and her embodiment of hope. From this basic framework, I draw out the function of hope in each woman's life and highlight the theological themes of each narrative.

The use of slave narratives as a theological source has both problems and advantages. One problem with antebellum narratives is that they were usually dictated to and written by whites. Narrative content could thus be affected by the editor's education, literary skills, religious beliefs, and attitude toward slavery. Generally speaking, antebellum editors were a group of professionals, such as lawyers, journalists, ministers, and teachers, who "had a great deal of prior experience in separating truth from fiction, applying rules of evidence, and accurately portraying men [and women] and events."[8]

The editor sometimes interjected his or her own views into the body of the narrative. At times, the narratives were very romantic and focused only on the flight from bondage. This characteristic is noted in the narratives of Ellenor Eldridge, Sally Williams, and Jane Blake. It is also possible that the editors felt greater liberty to romanticize narratives because they were dictated by women. Although abolitionist editors injected their own views and at times

---

7. William Jones, "Theodicy: The Controlling Category for Black Theology," in *Journal of Religious Thought* 30 (1973): 28–38.

8. John Blassingame, "Using the Testimony of Ex-Slaves: Approaches and Problems," in Davis and Gates, *The Slave's Narrative*, 79.

romanticized slavery, a comparison of the narratives with other historical documents of the era testifies to many of the factual details of their content.[9]

A further problem is that the small number of published antebellum narratives (around 106 autobiographical narratives before 1865) did not constitute a representative sample of the slave population. Some scholars, such as Ulrich B. Phillips, reject these accounts as being written by "exceptional slaves" who do not represent slaves as a class. Phillips readily accepts antebellum sources written by whites as "authentic" but has challenged the authenticity of most sources written by blacks because of the small number of sources. Historians, literary scholars, and theologians have verified the authenticity of slave narratives as a valuable source of knowledge regarding antebellum life. In conjunction with the small number of total narratives, the number of narratives by women is even smaller—just 12 percent of the total. Nonetheless, they remain our only access to slave women's lives as described by themselves and are of continuing importance. Though the selected narratives in this chapter do not necessarily constitute a representative sample, they are informative sources of black women's lives. The plethora of other antebellum sources, such as speeches, court records, journals, and letters, can verify that the published narratives accurately reflected, and sometimes softened, the female experiences of slavery.

While there are problems associated with using the slave narratives as a theological source, there are also several advantages. A major advantage of using autobiographical narratives is that these accounts are detailed accounts of the experiences of slavery. The antebellum narratives range from twenty pages to more than three hundred. Their length and detail facilitate discerning the patterns of discourse and experiences in these women's lives.[10] Another important insight gained from antebellum slave narratives is the divergent roots of black religious thinking in America. For example, they reveal that black women had their own distinctive interpretative key for understanding their lives religiously. They selectively appropriated the oppressor's religious tradition and formulated their own distinctive theology. The hush harbor meetings, spirituals, and prayers that form the backbone of black religiosity are recorded, in part, in slave narratives.[11]

A third advantage of having access to firsthand accounts of women's experiences is that the narratives give voice to the distinctive experience of women

---

9. Ibid., 82.

10. Ibid., 84.

11. A variety of works illustrate this point, such as Will Coleman, *Slave Narratives as a Source for a Contemporary Constructive Black Theology* (Ann Arbor, Mich.: University Microfilms International, 1993); Dwight Hopkins, *Cut Loose Your Stammering Tongue*; and Deborah Gray White, *Ar'n't I a Woman? Female Slaves in the Plantation South* (New York: W. W. Norton, 1985).

during slavery. Male narratives frequently alluded to the mistreatment of women, but they failed to illuminate the sexual vulnerability of slave women. They often lacked the descriptions of the passion, that is, the tenacity and courage of slave women. Perhaps most important of all, the narratives present and interpret women's experiences and the role of class, race, and gender oppression through their own voices. "The act of constructing a life narrative forces the author to move from accounts of discrete experience to an account of why and how the life took the shape it did."[12] The narratives provide black women's notions of oppression and their embodiment of hope.

Before we enter into dialogue with the four women who form the basis of the analysis that follows, a general introduction to each woman is appropriate. Details of their stories will unfold.

Mary Prince was born a slave on Brackish Pond in Bermuda. Her brief narrative, approximately twenty pages, reveals a life of almost constant physical and sexual abuse. Prince traveled extensively with her masters and experienced slavery in the West Indies, Spanish Port, Turks Island, Antigua, and England.

Born in Maryland in 1766, Old Elizabeth dictated her narrative at the age of ninety-seven, and it was subsequently published in 1863. Her narrative recounts her attempt to overcome her experience of abuse through religion, specifically through the struggle to find meaning in the atrocity of life as a slave.

Sojourner Truth was born a slave in 1797. She lived approximately half of her life in slavery in New York, and half as an emancipated black woman. Her narrative was first published in 1850. It was then republished in 1878 in her *Book of Life*, which includes her lectures and correspondence as a public figure. Her narrative chronicles the victimization of slavery and her religious sensibilities. Her book-length narrative details her life before, as well as after, she became an abolitionist, women's rights advocate, and preacher.

Harriet Jacobs's narrative, published in 1861, is one of the last autobiographical narratives by a slave woman published before the Civil War.[13] Jacobs, a mulatto, was born a slave to mulatto parents. Jacobs's narrative had the specific intent of exposing the sexual exploitation of slave women. Under the pseudonym of Linda Brent, Jacobs chronicled her journey from a victim of sexual exploitation to the communal effort that facilitated obtaining her freedom. Her religious understandings are secondary to her discussion of

---

12. Personal Narratives Group, ed., *Interpreting Women's Lives: Feminist Theory and Personal Narratives* (Bloomington: Indiana University Press, 1989), 4.

13. Valerie Smith, "Introduction" to Harriet Jacobs, *Incidents in the Live of a Slave Girl* (1861), repr. in Henry Louis Gates Jr., ed., *Six Women's Slave Narratives* (New York: Oxford University Press, 1988), xxvii.

exploitation, yet they elucidate the religious foundation of her passion for the possible in her life.

The conditions under which many black women were forced to exist were tolerated and perpetuated by whites due to the prevailing stereotypical myths about black people in general and black women in particular. These mythologies sanctioned the abuse of black women's bodies and legitimized their oppression. It is to a consideration of these mythologies that we must now turn.

Mythologies That Legitimized Abuse and Violence

Much of the racialized and sexualized ideology concerning black people pre-dates the establishment of this country. Blacks were depicted as irresponsible, puerile, docile, and promiscuous in literature as early as the 1600s.[14] The characterization of black women as sensual creatures dates back to early encounters between Englishmen, who were buying slaves, and Africans on the continent of Africa. The Englishmen mistook the seminudity of Africans—in response to the tropical climate—as lewdness. They also misappropriated the cultural tradition of polygamy as uncontrollable lust.[15] By 1736, African women were depicted in the *South Carolina Gazette* as having been able to serve their lovers "by night as well as day."[16] Even Thomas Jefferson espoused the sexualized mythologies concerning black women. He wrote that an orangutan preferred to mate with black women over the female of his own species.[17]

During slavery, the American mythologies regarding black persons in this country were molded into the American consciousness. The sexual exploitation of black women during slavery was undergirded by the earlier myths that

---

14. As White notes, Europeans who traveled to Africa recorded their superficial, uninformed analysis of African life. They made character judgment based on their faulty analysis. William Smith, after traveling to Africa, characterized black men as "orangutan like creatures [who] often attack and use violence to the Black women whenever they meet them alone in the woods." Smith described black women as "hot constitution'd Ladies" who were engaged in a continued quest for a lover. William Bosman described Guinea women as "fiery, warm, and so much hotter than the men." These sexualized mythologies soon extended to the Caribbean Islands and the Americas. From Jamaica emerged a poem dedicated to " 'The Sable Venus' in which sooty dames well vers'd in Venus' school, make love an art and boast they kiss by rule."

See William Smith, *A New Voyage to Guinea* (London: Frank Cass, 1967 [1744]), 51–52; William Bosman, *A New and Accurate Description of the Coast of Guinea* (London: Frank Cass, 1967 [1705]), 208–11; Winthrop D. Jordan, *White Over Black American Attitudes Toward the Negro, 1550–1812* (Chapel Hill: University of North Carolina Press, 1968), 150.

15. White, *Ar'n't I a Woman?*, 29.

16. *South Carolina Gazette*, 10 July 1736; quoted in White, *Ar'n't I a Woman?*, 30.

17. Merrill D. Peterson, ed., *The Portable Thomas Jefferson* (New York: Viking Press 1975), 187.

black women were licentious, rapacious, lustful animals. The term *negro wench* became a common, accepted reference to black women. Black women in antebellum America were depicted as being governed entirely by their libido. They were characterized as the Jezebels of the slave community.[18]

The *Jezebel mythology* concerning black women was the counterimage of white women. White women of the mid-nineteenth century were characterized as the Victorian ideal of true womanhood. White women were characterized as ladylike women who exercised "purity of conduct and purity of manners."[19] The "cult of true womanhood" encouraged submissiveness, domesticity, piety, and purity as its cardinal virtues. Any woman who could not adhere to these virtues was not a "true" woman. Tragically, black females were not seen as "women," let alone "true" women.

Some white women felt that black women were willing participants of rape rather than its victims.[20] Black women—not white men—were blamed for their victimization. The mythologies of the antebellum era did more than sexualize and racialize oppression toward black women. They undergirded the devaluation of black womanhood that permeated the psyche of American consciousness during slavery, emancipation, and even today.

The life and struggles of Harriet Jacobs elucidates this stereotypical mythology that undergirded the sexual oppression of slave women. Jacobs's narrative debunks the ideology that black women were immoral and lacked virtue. Her narrative demonstrates the character of life for black women in a social order that did not protect them from sexual exploitation. The early years of Jacobs's bondage were spent playing with her master's children. However, puberty brought a different experience. For Jacobs, and most female slaves, the fifteenth year was "a sad epoch in the life of a slave girl." At age fifteen, her master "began to whisper foul words in [her] ear. . . . He tried his utmost to corrupt

---

18. Jezebel was the wicked wife of King Ahab, who led him to sin against the God of Israel. See 1 Kings 16:18–21; 2 Kings 9.

19. White, *Ar'n't I a Woman?*, 39.

20. In the diary of Mary Boykin Chestnut, a Southern white woman, black women are called prostitutes who contribute to the compromise of white women's position in the home. She wrote:

(March 14, 1861) Under slavery, we (white women) live surrounded by prostitutes, yet an abandoned woman is sent out of any decent house. Who thinks any worse of a Negro or mulatto woman for being a thing we can't name? God, forgive us, but ours is a monstrous system, a wrong and an inequity! Like the patriarchs of old, our men live all in one house with their wives and their concubines; and the mulattoes one sees in every family partly resemble the white children. Any lady is ready to tell you who the father of all the mulatto children in everybody's household but her own. Those she thinks dropped from the clouds. My disgust is sometimes boiling over. Thank God for my country women, but alas for our men! They are probably no worse than men everywhere, but the lower the mistress, the more degraded they must be. *The Diary of Mary Boykin Chestnut*, 1861; quoted in bell hooks, *Ain't I a Woman? Black Women and Feminism* (Boston: South End Press, 1981), 53–54.

the pure principles [her] grandmother had instilled. He peopled [her] young mind with unclean images, such as only a vile monster could think of."[21]

In spite of the sexual harassment and exploitation, Jacobs, like other slave women, sought to maintain control over her own body. She understood herself as fully human (not property) and subject to God's will (not subject to the master's will). Like Jacobs, slave women clung tenaciously to the principles instilled in them by their mothers, aunts, grandmothers, or other females in their community in spite of the Jezebel mythology that undergirded their sexual exploitation.

Another myth regarding female slaves that developed during the time of slavery was that of *Mammy*. The Mammy myth characterized black women as docile, very religious, submissive, and asexual. Mammy was usually an older, overweight black woman who was the supervisor of her master's house. She was confidante and counselor to the white family, the spiritual influence and peacekeeper for the slaves. She was "harmless" and innocuous, just the opposite of Jezebel. The "harmlessness" of Mammy was translated by whites as powerlessness. Though "respected" and trusted enough to work in the house, Mammy did not have the power to stop the exploitation of female slaves. Black women who worked in the "big house" were often sexual objects, conveniently located in the house, for the master's use. Both of these mythologies, Mammy and Jezebel, legitimized the abuse and violence perpetrated against black women. They undergirded the evil and suffering that prompted black women to record their struggles, as well as their hopes, in their narratives.

The Impetus to Write

The racialized and sexualized violence that black women were forced to endure during enslavement prompted them to reclaim their personhood through the pen. Slave women *wrote themselves into being* through their narratives. The narratives were an act of self-creation. They were a response and a rebuttal to the claim that blacks *could not* write. In her narrative, published in 1866, Missouri slave Mattie Jackson admonished female slaves to learn to read and write in order to "manage your own secrets, divulge them by the silent language of your own pen."[22] The mastery of language and writ-

---

21. Jacobs, *Incidents in the Life of a Slave Girl*, 44.

22. L. S. Thompson, *The Story of Mattie Jackson: Her Parentage, Experience of Eighteen Years of Slavery, Incidents During the War, Her Escape; A True Story as Given by Mattie* (1866); repr. in Gates, ed., *Six Women's Slave Narratives*, 29.

ing was equated with personhood and presence. A black person became human through the mastery of language. The slaves were eyewitnesses and I-witnesses to the atrocities of slavery.[23] Through their narratives, slave women voiced their experience of the monstrous, abusive system. Black women seized the authority to speak for themselves through their pens.

Mary Prince wrote her narrative so that "the good people in England might hear from a slave what a slave had felt and suffered."[24] Prince suffered severe whippings and extremely cruel treatment from her masters who "had no heart—no fear of God." For Prince, telling her story bonded her with the sufferings of other slaves. She declared that "in telling my own sorrows, I cannot pass by those of my fellow slaves—for when I think of my grief I remember theirs."[25]

In Maria Stewart's narrative, she noted the personal ramifications of publishing the plight of the slave. Stewart was born free in 1803, orphaned at age five, and "bound out" in a clergyman's family. Stewart noted in her autobiographical narrative, published in 1835, "[m]any will suffer for pleading the cause of oppressed Africa, and I shall glory in being one of her martyrs, for I am firmly persuaded that the God in whom I trust is able to protect me from the rage and malice of mine enemies, and from them that will rise up against me; and if there is no other way for me to escape, he is able to take me to himself."[26] For Stewart, a free woman, slavery was communal subjugation that they impinged upon the lives of all black people. She was willing to be its martyr, if necessary, to fight for freedom. A major impetus for her narrative and her subsequent political writings was the lynching of blacks, both women and men.

Sojourner Truth wrote her narrative to claim her personhood. Historian Nell Painter asserts that "the *Narrative of Sojourner Truth* marks a turning point in the biography of Sojourner Truth—her first step into deliberate representation of self."[27] The motivations for writing were varied, but a consistent theme is the desire to speak for oneself about her own experiences. This speaking affirmed the presence, humanity, self-perception, and faith of the authors.

The narratives of women were also written to expose the distinctive nature of black women's victimization. Primarily, the oppression of slave women was through violence to their bodies. Violence took various forms, including whipping, rape, sexual abuse, exposure of their genitalia or private body parts,

23. Davis and Gates, *The Slave's Narrative*, xxxii.

24. Ibid., iii.

25. Ibid., 12.

26. Maria Stewart, "Productions of Maria Stewart" (1835); repr. in Henry Louis Gates Jr., ed., *Spiritual Narratives* (New York: Oxford University Press, 1988), 5.

27. Nell Painter, *Sojourner Truth: A Life, a Symbol* (New York: W. W. Norton, 1996), 110.

physical deprivation, and mutilation. The suffering of slave women highlights the convergence of race, gender, and class oppression. These slaves were victims of whites, old or young, male or female, because they were black, poor, and female.

Harriet Jacobs, a North Carolina slave born in 1815 to a mulatto couple, boldly chronicles in her narrative the multidimensional oppression of black women in slavery. She asserted that slavery was terrible for men, "but it was far more terrible for women. Superadded to the burden common to all, *they* [women] have wrongs, and sufferings, and mortifications peculiarly their own."[28] Her narrative was written for the specific purpose of exposing the abuse of slave women. Writing under the pseudonym Linda Brent, she noted in her narrative, *Incidents in the Life of a Slave Girl: Written by Herself*, that "[no] pen can give an adequate description of the all pervading corruption produced by slavery. The slave girl is reared in an atmosphere of licentiousness and fear. . . . it needs an abler pen than mine to describe the extremity of their suffering, the depths of their degradation. . . ."[29]

Jacobs's narrative, published in 1861, is centered on the sexual exploitation of female slaves. The gender analysis is central in the overall content of the narrative. *Incidents* is the "only slave narrative that takes as its subject the sexual exploitation of female slaves"—thus the narrative centers on sexual oppression as well as the oppression of race and condition of existence. Further, the narrative is written specifically to a female audience to warn of and expose the horrors of slavery.[30]

Sexual exploitation, Jacobs asserted, was exacerbated by beauty. "If God has bestowed beauty upon her, it will prove her greatest curse. That which commands admiration in the white woman only hastens the degradation of the female slave."[31] Jacobs experienced the degradation of slavery through the relentless sexual pursuit of her master, who she said to her knowledge had fathered eleven slaves.[32] "My master met me at every turn, reminding me that I belonged to him, and swearing by heaven and earth that he would compel me to submit to him. If I went out for a breath of fresh air, after a day of unwearied toil, his footsteps dogged me. If I knelt by my mother's grave, his dark shadow fell upon me there. The light heart which nature had given me became heavy with sad forebodings."[33] Jacobs hid for seven years in the crawl space

---

28. Jacobs, *Incidents in the Life of a Slave Girl*, 119.
29. Ibid.
30. Yellin, "Text and Context of Harriet Jacobs' *Incidents*," 263.
31. Jacobs, *Incidents in the Life of a Slave Girl*, 46.
32. Ibid., 55.
33. Ibid., 46.

of her grandmother's house in order to escape her master's sexual advances.[34] The crawl space was nine feet long, seven feet wide, and three feet high. Though her grandmother's house was "practically in her master's backyard," he never found her. She later escaped to New York[35] and eventually her freedom was purchased.[36]

Sexual abuse and violence permeated the life of Mary Prince. Abused and violated for the slightest offense, she was pinched, whipped, stripped naked, and abused by master and mistress. "To strip me naked—to hang me up by the wrists and lay my flesh open with the cowskin—was an ordinary punishment for even a slight offense."[37] Prince recalled a beating she received from her master, Mister I_____, for accidentally breaking an earthen jar that was already cracked. When Mister I_____ returned home and was informed by his wife that the jar had been broken, he abused Mary verbally and physically. He hit her several times with his hands and promised to beat her in the morning. He kept his promise. "He tied me upon a ladder, and gave me a hundred lashes with his own hand, and Master Benjy stood by to count for him. When he had licked me for some time, he sat down to take a breath; then after resting, he beat me again and again and again until he was quite wearied, and so hot (for the weather was very sultry) that he sank back in his chair, almost like to faint. . . . my mistress went to bring him a drink."[38]

Mary Prince's mistress, Mrs. I_____, also abused her mercilessly. Her second day as Mrs. I_____'s slave, she recalled: "She caused me to know the exact difference between the smart of the rope, the cart whip, and the cowskin, when applied to my naked body by her own cruel hand. And there was scarcely any punishment more dreadful than the blows I received on my face and head from her heavy fist. She was a dreadful woman, and a savage mistress to her slaves."[39]

Slave women in the North also suffered the sexualized and racialized violence that southern slave women were forced to endure, as we know from Sojourner Truth's *Narrative*. Truth's *Narrative* is a dictated autobiography written in 1850 by white abolitionist Olive Gilbert. The 1850 edition chronicles the

---

34. Ibid., 224.
35. New York became a free state in 1827. Blacks born in the state before 1799 were freed. The fugitive slave law enacted in the North encouraged the return of escaped slaves to their masters in the South. Slaves had to purchase their freedom in order to avoid being returned to their master as a runaway. See Jacobs, *Incidents in the Life of a Slave Girl*, 285–92.
36. Jacobs, *Incidents in the Life of a Slave Girl*, 26–27; 97–151.
37. Thomas Pringle, ed., *History of Mary Prince; Related by Herself* (1831); repr. in Gates, ed., *Six Women's Slave Narratives*, 7.
38. Ibid., 8.
39. Ibid., 6.

life of the slave child, Isabella, through the transformative process of becoming Sojourner Truth, abolitionist and public speaker. Truth's *Narrative* "is a classic slave narrative recounting the abuse and dislocation of slavery and providing justification for her escape and later career as an abolitionist."[40] The *Narrative* was reprinted in 1878 along with *The Book of Life*, a compilation of correspondence and biographical sketches of Truth's life.

Truth (named Isabella at birth) was born in 1797 in Ulster County, New York, to slave parents. Her parents were owned by a Dutch-speaking family; thus, Dutch was Isabella's primary language. Though one of ten to twelve children born to her parents, Isabella knew only one of her siblings. The others had been sold, auctioned off like horses, cattle, or any other property.

After the death of her parents' master, Charles Hendenberg (1807 or 1808), all of his property, including his slaves, was auctioned off. Nine-year-old Isabella was torn from her parents and her brother and sold for one hundred dollars to Mr. John Nealy. Isabella recorded in her narrative the pain of a life as chattel. The slave auction, she notes, "is a terrible affair to its victims, and its incidents and consequences are graven on their hearts with a pen of burning steel."[41] Isabella labeled this the beginning of her "trials of life."

The language barrier between the English-speaking Nealys and Dutch-speaking Isabella proved to be an additional source of oppression for Isabella. She was whipped severely because she often did not understand what her master requested of her. She was once sent to get a skillet and returned with a pothook. Her master "whipped her till the flesh was deeply lacerated, and the blood streamed from her wounds—and the scars remained (till her death) to testify of that fact."[42]

The sexual abuse of Sojourner Truth has been "passed over in silence."[43] Her narrative implies that she was not only sexually abused by her master, but she was also the sexual object of her mistress.[44] She noted that many incidents were not recorded "because they [were] not at all for the public ear by their

---

40. Henry Louis Gates Jr., ed., *Narrative of Sojourner Truth: A Bondswoman of Olden Time, with a History of Her Labors and Correspondence Drawn from Her "Book of Life"* (New York: Oxford University Press, 1991), xxxvii.

41. Ibid., 30.

42. Ibid., 26.

43. Ibid., 30.

44. Nell Painter discusses the allusion to sexual abuse of Sojourner by her mistress, Sally Dumont. To mention rape by slave masters was not uncommon in slave narratives, and the physical abuse was clearly explicated, so Painter suggests that this was an untalked-about incident of a woman sexually abusing another woman. Painter references another incident in which Sojourner is the sexual object of the wife of a cult leader, Prophet Mathasis, that Sojourner became involved with after her emancipation, before her preaching/lecturing career began. See Painter, *Sojourner Truth*, 16, 56.

very nature . . . so unreasonable, so unnatural they would not be easily believed."[45] However, her narrative does give a glimpse of the physical and sexual abuse endured by many slave women, as well as the resistance, determination, and hope they possessed.

The first paragraph of Old Elizabeth's narrative records that she was born in 1766 to slave parents who were "religious people." She immediately moves to an incident of violence that is paradigmatic and the impetus for writing her narrative. She articulates the interconnectedness between her faith and her experiences of racialized and sexualized violence. Her narrative relates an incident that occurred at age eleven after she was sold away from her mother and siblings. She ran away from her plantation to visit her family and upon returning to the plantation her master severely whipped her. She noted, "He tied me with a rope, and gave me some stripes of which I carried the marks for weeks."[46] She recalled her mother's parting words to her that she had "nobody in the world to look to but God."[47] Her narrative focuses on her determination to be the empowered woman that God ordained her to be in spite of oppression from the whole community.

These slave women's narratives tell of the horrors and atrocities of daily life in bondage. Yet, in the midst of their Holler, a hope emerges. They show black women's understanding of God's presence in the midst of trial and tribulation, and give voice to the slave's understanding of God's care, love, and faithfulness when no one else could be counted on.

Though the hope posited in a narrative is but one voice (the writer or speaker), it integrates the communal and individual hope employed to negotiate or transcend victimization. African American women's narratives transcend preoccupation with individualism. The self is a member of an oppressed social group with concerns, responsibilities to, and hopes for the community.[48] From the bowels of slavery, black women expressed an undauntable hope, a passion for the possible in their lives.

---

45. Painter, *Sojourner Truth*, 81–82.

46. "Memoirs of Old Elizabeth, a Colored Woman," in *Six Women's Slave Narratives*, ed. Henry Louis Gates. Originally published in 1863 by Collins Printer (New York: Oxford University Press, 1988), 4.

47. Ibid.

48. Stephen Butterfield, *Black Autobiography in America* (Amherst: University of Massachusetts Press, 1974), 1, 3, 4. He is one of several scholars who have researched the characteristics of autobiography. He cites the communal consciousness as one of the salient characteristics of African American women's autobiographies. Cf. James Craig Holte, *The Ethnic I: A Sourcebook for Ethnic-American Autobiography* (New York: Greenwood House, 1988), 3; Roger Rosenblatt, "Black Autobiography: Life as the Death Weapon" in *Autobiography: Essays Theoretical and Critical*, ed. James Olney (Princeton, N.J.: Princeton University Press, 1980).

The Roots of Hope

Slaves' hope was rooted in their experiences of slavery and their relationship with God. The slaves' religion was an undergirding stabilizer that enabled them to hope. In the "invisible institution"—the snatched-out sacred spaces where the slaves worshiped—they prayed, sang, and testified about the goodness of the Lord even in the midst of bondage. From the invisible institution crafted in the throes of oppression came a distinctive understanding of the slave's faith in God and God's care of oppressed people.

Slaves were not passive victims of white oppression. From 1619 through the end of the Civil War, slaves developed, molded, and shaped a world and worldview separate from those of their masters. Sometimes their world was visible to the master, but it was usually incomprehensible. Often the slave's world was totally invisible to the master. In the bush arbor, the woods, or the slave quarters, slaves crafted a community and a distinctive theology. Slaves sang, danced, prayed, and shared their meager material resources with one another. They cared for one another's wounds and reared one another's children. They were a bonded people in spite of their adverse situation. Slaves' hidden religious gatherings forged resistance and survival strategies. These resistance strategies enabled them to maintain their dignity and support the moral, familial, and religious dimensions of their slave community.

A major resistance strategy developed by slaves was counter-cultural theology. In using the term *counter-cultural theology*, I am asserting that slaves appropriated and applied Scripture according to their own understanding of, or engagement with, the Bible, and their interpretations often countered the theology of the dominant, oppressive culture. Usually their understanding followed more closely the literal statements of the Bible rather than the slave master's interpretation of Scripture. Religion was not an opiate to soothe the brutalities of slavery. It was the fire that ignited the passion for justice and full humanity. This slave theology changed the traditional understanding of theology in the white community to a theology of love, compassion, humanity, and care for the slave. In this counter-cultural theology, white people were held accountable to God for their sins and the sins they forced upon black people. For example, Mary Prince understood the Sabbath in the biblical sense, and she applied the concept differently to the lives of slaves than to the slave master. It is very wrong, she notes, "to work on Sunday or to go to market; but will not God call the Buckra (white) men to answer for this on the great day of judgment—since they will give slaves no other day?"[49] She anticipated

---

49. *History of Mary Prince*, 16.

God's grace toward slaves forced to violate the Sabbath and judgment toward the slave master who put them in this position. Slaves' counter-cultural theology contextualized their religion.

Sojourner Truth expounded even more on the counter-cultural theology that emerged during slavery. She distinguished between what she named the "religion of Jesus" and the "religion of America." The religion of Jesus affirmed slaves as humans, while the religion of America treated them like cattle. The religion of Jesus was life-giving, while the religion of America was "soul-killing." The religion of Jesus diametrically opposed the institution of slavery and the oppression of women, while the religion of America, through its participation and silence, sanctioned both.[50] In the early stages of Sojourner's counter-cultural development, she noted that in the "religion of America" the slave master "was as a God. He knew of and could see her at all times, even as God himself"[51] saw all and controlled all. She would voluntarily confess her sins to her master "from the conviction that he already knew them."[52] But as she matured and experienced life, her theology changed. At a women's rights convention in Akron, Ohio, in 1851, she responded to a white man's contention that because Jesus was a male, women (meaning white women) could not have the same rights as men. Sojourner replied, "[w]here did Christ come from? Christ came from God and a woman. Man had nothing to do with him."[53] For Sojourner, her understanding of Scripture was a corrective to the theology of America that negated women and blacks.

It is significant that Sojourner places her discussion of the religion of America and the religion of Jesus in the middle of the discussion of her marriage. The religion of America victimized black women's bodies in another way. It denied slaves the legal right to choose their mates. Marriages between slaves were often performed by other slaves because "no true minister of Christ (could) perform in the presence of God what they know to be mere farce . . . unrecognized (marriage) by civil law."[54] Further, these marriages were subject to annulment at any time the interest or the caprices of god (the slave master) dictated. Sojourner was not allowed to marry the slave she loved but was married to a slave who had been sold two other times and required to take a wife by each new master.

Harriet Jacobs also differentiated between the "religion of the South" and Christianity. She noted: "There is a great difference between Christianity and

---

50. Gates, ed., *Narrative of Sojourner Truth*, 36.
51. Ibid., 33.
52. Ibid.
53. Ibid., 134–35.
54. Ibid., 36–37.

the religion of the South. If a man goes to the communion table, and pays money into the treasury of the church, no matter if it be the price of blood, he is called religious. If a pastor has offspring by a woman not his wife, the church dismisses him, if she is a white woman, but if she is colored, it does not hinder him from being their good Shepherd."[55] Jacobs understood that in the "religion of the South" the life and bodily integrity of the slave were totally ignored. Money donated to the church from the sale of humans was readily accepted, while humans conceived out of this monstrous system were quickly rejected.

The religion of the South often did not allow slaves to attend church. Jacobs asserted that the slaves wanted to hear the gospel and attend church but were forgotten, overlooked, or deemed too ignorant to understand the word of God:

> There are thousands who . . . are thirsting for the water of life, but the law forbids it, and the churches withhold it. They send the Bible to heathen abroad, and neglect the heathen at home. . . . Talk to the American slave holders as you talk to savages in Africa. Tell *them* it is wrong to traffic in men. Tell them it is sinful to sell their own children, and atrocious to violate their own daughters. Tell them that all men are brethren, and that man has no right to shut out the light of knowledge from his brothers. Tell them they are answerable to God for stealing the Fountain of Life from souls that are thirsting for it.[56]

Jacobs posed a critical question to the religious leaders of the North who failed to make a prophetic critique of the dehumanizing, un-Christian terror of slavery. She asked, "Are doctors of divinity blind, or are they hypocrites?" The Northern clergymen seemed too quickly blinded to the atrocities of slavery. The slaveholders showed them their land, their cattle, their gardens, and their comfortable homes, and invited them to talk with the favored household slaves. "The southerner invites him to talk with them. He asks them if they want to be free, and they say, 'o, no, massa' and that is enough to satisfy him. He comes home to publish 'A Southern View of Slavery,' and to complain of the exaggeration of abolitionists. He assures his people that he has been to the south and seen slavery for himself, that is a beautiful 'patriarchal institution,' that the slaves don't want freedom, that they have hallelujah meetings and other religious privileges."[57] Rather than his conversion having a positive effect on her master's treatment of his slaves, Jacobs noted that he was even

---

55. Jacobs, *Incidents in the Life of a Slave Girl*, 115.
56. Ibid., 113.
57. Ibid., 114.

more cruel after his conversion. Like Sojourner Truth's master, Jacobs's master felt that *he* was God in her life. The following conversation between Jacobs and her master illustrates this graphically:

> "You can do what I require [submit to his sexual advances], and if you are faithful to me, you will be as virtuous as my wife," he replied. I answered that the Bible didn't say so. His voice became hoarse with rage. "How dare you preach about *your* infernal Bible," he exclaimed. "What right have you, who are my Negro, to talk to me about what you would like, and what you wouldn't like? I am your master, you shall obey me." No wonder the slaves sing, "Ole Satan's church is here below: Up to God's free church I hope to go."[58]

Slaves refused to succumb to the oppressive, dehumanizing religion of the South. Jacobs's master's reference to "your infernal Bible" suggests that he had discerned that the slaves' religion, and their appropriation of the Bible, was different from his.

Jacobs's experiences of slavery evoked her response regarding mistreatment by her "Christian" mistress. She noted that she was taught by her mistresses: "Thou shall love thy neighbor as thyself." But Jacobs said, "I was her slave, and I supposed she did not recognize me as her neighbor."[59] Jacobs's theology validated her as one to be treated humanely, to be loved, and to be recognized as "neighbor."

The religion of the South denied Jacobs the right to marry. Jacobs fell in love with a free black man, a carpenter, who proposed marriage to her. Because she was a slave and knew the law would not recognize her marriage, she refused to marry him. She wrote, "I loved him with all the ardor of a young girl's first love. But when I reflected that I was a slave, and that the laws gave no sanction to the marriage of such, my heart sank within me. My lover wanted to buy me, but I knew that Dr. Flint was too skillful and arbitrary a man to consent to that arrangement."[60] In the religion of the South, even marriage would not shield Jacobs from the sexual advances of her master because "the husband of a slave had no power to protect her."[61] Jacobs resolved herself to her plight after Dr. Flint refused permission for her to marry the man she loved, struck her (the first time he had ever hit her), and threatened to shoot her lover. Jacobs concluded:

---

58. Ibid., 115–16 (brackets and italics mine).
59. Ibid., 16.
60. Ibid., 58–59.
61. Ibid., 59.

My lover was an intelligent and religious man. Even if he could not have
obtained permission to marry me while I was a slave, the marriage would
give him no power to protect me from my master. It would have made him
miserable to witness the insults I should have been subjected to. And then
if we had children, I knew they must "follow the condition of the mother."
What a terrible blight that would be on the heart of a free intelligent father!
For *his* sake I felt I ought not link him with my own unhappy destiny. . . . I
earnestly entreated him not to come back. I advised him to go to the Free
States. . . .[62]

Insulted that Jacobs had chosen her own mate, Dr. Flint offered her the opportunity to marry one of his slaves. Jacobs remained unmarried.

According to Jacobs's theology, she had the right to determine the use of
her body, even if it defied what was considered prudent for her day. Years later,
in a defiant act of resistance and determination not to submit to the advances
of Dr. Flint, Jacobs sacrificed her own self-respect in the eyes of her grandmother and community by taking a white man as her lover. For her "it seemed
less degrading to give one's self, than to submit to compulsion. There [was]
something akin to freedom in having a lover who has no control over you,
except that which he gains by kindness and attachment."[63] Jacobs preferred
this act of freedom over the hypocrisy of laws and religion that dehumanized
slave women and denied them the God-given right to choose a mate.

The abuses of slavery made it poignantly clear that there was no one to rely
on but Jesus and God. The religion of America denied Old Elizabeth unhin-
dered worship in the church, but the religion of Jesus enabled her to "have
church" wherever she was. Old Elizabeth found "she had none to look to but
God" so she "betook" herself to prayer. She notes, "In every lonely place [she]
found an altar." She prayed in the corner of the fields, under the fences, or
anywhere the Spirit moved her to pray.[64] Her spirit was taught how to pray,
"Lord, have mercy on me—Christ save me." She was sustained by an "invisible power" that told her "that all the hope she had of being saved was no more
than a (single strand of) hair, still pray, and it would be sufficient."[65] In spite
of the trials and tribulations of slavery, Old Elizabeth embodied the religion
of Jesus and the hope of female slaves. Hope, the size of a single strand of
hair, was enough to sustain her from oppression to freedom.

The early portion of Mary Prince's narrative makes only two references

---

62. Ibid., 65–66.
63. Ibid., 84–85.
64. *Memoir of Old Elizabeth*, 4.
65. Ibid., 5–6.

to God's care or God's presence in her situation of extreme victimization. It was after she attended a Methodist prayer meeting on another plantation that her religious life took on meaning for her. The prayer meeting was led by women. She had heard the "religion of America" from her own slave master, but the prayers at this meeting were different. She noted: "They were the first prayers I ever understood. One woman prayed; and then they sung a hymn; . . . then they all spoke of their own grief as sinners. . . . I felt grieved at my own sins also. I cried the whole night, but was too much ashamed to speak. I prayed to God to forgive me."[66] She was led to seek religious instruction in the Moravian Church. It is significant that the religion of Jesus led slaves, who were oppressed, beaten, starved, and raped, to ask forgiveness for their "sins." Yet, the religion of America justified, or at least callused the consciences of those who claimed to be Christian and at the same time abused the "least of these."

Prince's mistress would not allow her to attend instruction classes at the church. "I did not tell my mistress about it; for I knew that she would not give me leave to go. But I felt I *must* go. . . . I wished at the time to attend a Sunday school taught by Mr. Curtin, but he would not receive me without a written note from my master, granting permission"[67] which she knew she would never get.

Sojourner Truth, who was enslaved in the North, named this counter-cultural theology the *Religion of America*, while Jacobs, who was enslaved in the South, called it the *Religion of the South*. Perhaps Sojourner poignantly understood, through her own experiences, that the atrocities of slavery, the victimization of black women's bodies, and the denial of basic human and legal rights were not limited to the South.

In each of the selected narratives, a counter-cultural theology emerges. These women lived their theology, as well as wrote and preached about it. Slave women's counter-cultural theology contained a radical incarnational anthropology that resisted oppression, and fought for justice and human liberation just as Jesus, the living Word, did. It is radical because slaves' religious understanding and ways of existing in the society deviated strongly from the dominant culture. Because of the presence of God inside them (incarnation), slave women were courageous enough to holler and yet resist oppression. Their counter-cultural theology undergirded their passionate quest for voice, humanity, and the freedom to control their lives and bodies.

---

66. *History of Mary Prince*, 16.
67. Ibid., 16–17.

The Contours of Hope

In the counter-cultural theology found in the narratives of slave women, passion for the possible in their lives—voice, humanity, and freedom—was the slave woman's hope. Hope for these women was not primarily an eschatological notion seeking fulfillment in the ultimate kingdom of God. Rather, hope had a strong this-worldly function that countered the this-worldly abuse and victimization of slavery. Nevertheless, their hope was not a purely human construct; it was grounded in belief in a God who aids the oppressed of humanity.

The narratives of these slave women demonstrates the *maldistribution* of abuse meted out upon black women. Their experiences of abuse were the daily experiences of most female slaves.[68] The whippings, sexual abuse, and denial of basic human rights, such as the right to choose one's mate, or the freedom of worship, elucidate the *severity* and dehumanizing effects of slavery. The *transgenerational* character of abuse and violence is implied in the very fact that these women were born into the institution of slavery. Their mothers, sisters, aunts, and grandmothers had suffered the same atrocities. Many of these women wrote as mothers and grandmothers who had seen their children endure the abuses of slavery. Black women's *hope*, however, is the mirror image of their distinctive suffering. It too is maldistributed, enormous, and transgenerational. In the narrative of Mattie Jackson, which was dictated in 1865, she challenged all women to seize voice by writing their "own secrets." She managed her secrets by seizing voice in her narrative, and revealing the abuse and violence she endured. Her master "was a very severe and cruel master, and inflicted such punishment upon us as he thought proper."[69] She chronicled her family's separation and their untiring quest for freedom. Rather than allowing her master to sell him away from the family, Mattie's husband escaped to the Free States. She noted "though the parting was painful, it afforded her solace in the contemplation of her husband becoming a free man, and cherishing a hope that her little family, through the aid of some angel of mercy, might be enabled to escape also, and meet to part no more on earth."[70] Her mother was the last in her family to be freed. "After so many long years

---

68. See, for instance, Bert James Loewenberg and Ruth Bogin, *Black Women in Nineteenth Century American Life: Their Words, Their Thoughts, Their Feelings* (University Park: Pennsylvania State University Press, 1976); White, *Ar'n't I a Woman?*; Dorothy Sterling, ed., *We Are Your Sisters: Black Women in the Nineteenth Century* (New York: W. W. Norton, 1984); Albert Octavia V. Rogers, *House of Bondage, or, Charlotte Brooks and Other Slaves* (New York: Oxford University Press, 1988 [1890]).

69. *Story of Mattie Jackson*, 10.

70. Ibid., 8.

and so many attempts, for this was her seventh, she at last succeeded, and we were all free. My mother had been a slave for more than forty-three years, and liberty was very sweet to her."[71] (She used the same metaphor, *freedom is sweet*, that Mary Prince used.) Jackson ended her narrative by expressing the faith that undergirded her hope. She discussed her understanding of the Word of God:

> It provides light for this darkness, joy for this anguish, a solace for his woes, balm for his wounds, and heaven for his hopes. It unveils the unseen world, and reveals him who is light of creation, and joy of the universe, reconciled through the death of His Son. It promises the faithful a blessed re-union in a land undimmed with tears, unmarked by sorrow. It affords a truth for the living and a refuge for the dying. Aided by the Holy Spirit, it guides us through life, points out the shoals, the quicksand hidden rocks which endanger our path, and at last leaves us with the eternal God our refuge, and his everlasting arms of protection.[72]

Jackson's testimony is typical of the narratives of slavery. Like the narratives of Old Elizabeth, Jacobs, Sojourner, and Prince, it chronicles the *maldistributed* passion for humanity, freedom, and voice that rested upon the faith of slave women.

Harriet Jacobs's narrative demonstrates the *enormity* of slave women's hope. Slave women's passion for freedom was undiminished by adverse circumstances. When Jacobs learned that her children would be held as slaves for her master's daughter, she risked all to escape to freedom and secure her children. "Providence opened an unexpected way for me to escape."[73] She recalled the years of hiding in the small garret of her grandmother's house:

> For the last time I went up to my nook. Its desolate look no longer chilled me, for the light of hope had risen in my soul. Yet, even with the blessed prospects of freedom before me, I felt very sad at leaving forever the old homestead, where I had been sheltered so long by my grandmother, where I had dreamed my first dream of love, and where after that had faded away, my children came to twine themselves so closely round my desolate heart. As the hour approached for me to leave, I again descended to the store-room. My grandmother and Benny [her brother] were there. She took my hand, and said, "Linda, let us pray." We knelt down together, while my child heart, and my other arm around the faithful, loving old friend I was about to leave forever. On no other occasion has it ever been my lot to

---

71. Ibid., 32.
72. Ibid., 41–42.
73. Jacobs, *Incidents in the Life of a Slave Girl*, 227.

listen to such fervent a supplication for mercy and protection. It thrilled through my heart, and inspired me with trust in God. Peter [a friend] was waiting for me in the street. I was soon by his side, faint in body, but strong in purpose.[74]

After escaping to freedom, she risked her life, her freedom, and all her resources to return for her children.[75]

The *transgenerational* character of hope was also attested to in the slave women's narratives. Harriet Jacobs's passion for the possible in her life was fueled by her father's teaching that she was fully human. The slave master asserted that her father "spoiled his children, by teaching them to feel that they were human beings. This was a blasphemous doctrine for a slave to teach; presumptuous in him, and dangerous to the master."[76] Jacobs's grandmother also instilled words of faith and hope in her. Jacobs was "indebted to her for all [her] comforts, spiritual or temporal," Jacobs noted.[77] Though her grandmother had come to accept slavery as the "fate of black people," she lived the religion of Jesus:

> Most earnestly did she [her grandmother] strive to make us feel that it was the will of God: that He had seen fit to place us under such circumstances; and though it (slavery) seemed hard, we ought to pray for contentment.
>
> It was a beautiful faith, coming from a mother who could not call her children her own. But I, and Benjamin (her youngest boy), condemned it. We reasoned that it was much more the will of God that we should be situated as she was. We longed for a home like hers. There we always found sweet balsam for our troubles. She was so loving, so sympathizing! She always met us with a smile, and listened with patience to all our sorrows. She spoke so hopefully, that unconsciously the clouds gave place to sunshine.[78]

Jacobs condemned a passive acceptance of fate and adopted a faith that empowered her to resist the abuses of slavery. Her hope was grounded in the presence of God in her life and the knowledge that she was one of God's children.

Theological seeds of hope were planted in Isabella (Sojourner Truth) by her mother. She taught Isabella that if she asked God out loud for whatever she needed, God would be with her and provide for her. In the hours of oppression and extremity, "she did not forget the instruction of her mother, to go to God in all her trials and every affliction: and she not only remembered, but obeyed:

---

74. Ibid., 235–36.
75. Ibid.
76. Ibid., 18–19.
77. Ibid., 19.
78. Ibid., 28–29.

going to him, 'and telling him all and asking Him if He thought it was right,' and begging him to protect and shield her from her persecutors. She always asked with unwavering faith that she should receive just what she plead for."[79] It was out of this transgenerational faith that God directed, protected her, and empowered her to untiringly strive for human dignity, freedom, and voice.

Isabella believed that God assisted and directed her escape from slavery. After her master refused to give her the "free papers" on July 4, 1827, as he had promised, Isabella decided to take her freedom into her own hands. Like Mary, the mother of Jesus, she pondered the saying in her heart. She "determined inwardly" that she would remain with her master for a short while, to finish the heavy fall work of spinning the wool, then escape to freedom.[80]

Old Elizabeth was "born to religious parents." The principles instilled in her during her childhood inform the subsequent developments of her life. Eventually, she became a powerful itinerant preacher.[81] Her passion for freedom, and her power to preach against the objections of whites, was rooted in the religious principles instilled in her by her parents.

In addition to the distinctive character of black women's hope that is posited in their narratives, I have argued that their hope was a theological, as opposed to merely psychological or social, concept of hope. Slave women's hope was rooted in their counter-cultural theology, which had strong christological and pneumatological dimensions. One way that this is expressed is in the tendency to liken themselves to biblical characters and compare their experiences to biblical stories. Jesus was their hermeneutical key for interpreting life and the impetus for seeking freedom (Christology). Slave women knew Jesus as the one who understood their suffering, because, like them, he had suffered and been mistreated. Jesus was an innocent victim of the religious leaders, the wealthy, and the masses in general, as were the slaves. He was ridiculed, humiliated, struck in the face, whipped, displayed naked on the cross, and dehumanized, as they were. Jesus knew all their troubles. Old Elizabeth asserted that her preaching ministry was rejected, like Jesus' ministry. She noted, "I endeavored to keep silence; but I could not quench the Spirit. I was rejected by the elders and rulers, as Christ was rejected by the Jews before me. . . ."[82]

For Sojourner Truth, there was but one message that needed to be preached—Jesus. Sojourner exclaimed, "I journeys round about to the camp meetin's, an' wherever folks is. . . . I sing an' then folks always comes up round me, an' then

79. Gates, ed., *Narrative of Sojourner Truth*, 27.
80. Ibid., 41–43.
81. *Memoir of Old Elizabeth*, 7.
82. Ibid., 13.

I preaches to 'em. I tell 'em about Jesus, an' I tell 'em about the sins of this people."[83] Jesus was the redeemer and sustainer over the "sins of this people."

Like the biblical characters Jacob, Abram, and Sarai, Sojourner Truth wanted God to give her a new name. It was after her emancipation from slavery that Isabella's name was changed to Sojourner Truth. Her life as abolitionist and orator has been widely written about. However, it is out of the faith born in slavery and the experiences of dehumanization and abuse—physical and sexual, whippings, rape, being used as a sexual object, denial of basic human rights—that Sojourner Truth, preacher, teacher, women's rights advocate, and public speaker, emerges. Sojourner was not content to wait to "get a new name in glory"; she wanted one now. The changing of her name was an act of the Lord, according to Sojourner, indicative of the direction and calling God had placed upon her life. "My name was Isabella; but when I left the house of bondage, I left everything behind. I wa'n't goin' to keep nothin' of Egypt on me, an' so I went to the Lord an' asked him to give me a new name. And the Lord gave me Sojourner because I was to travel up an' down the land, showin' the people their sins, an' bein' a sign unto them. Afterward I told the Lord I wanted another name, 'cause everybody else had two names; and the Lord gave me Truth because I was to declare the truth to the people."[84] Isabella marked her movement from slavery to freedom through claiming a new name indicative of her faith, the God presence, and direction for her life. Her faith was the foundation of her role as abolitionist and orator during emancipation. Her gospel was women's rights and the love of Jesus that provided freedom and humanity for all.

The slave master and mistress thought it was demonic, rather than Christ inspired, for the slaves to desire freedom. When Prince requested permission to buy her own freedom, her mistress, Mrs. Woods, became outraged at the very idea. Mrs. Woods told Prince she was a "black devil" and insisted on knowing who had "planted the idea of freedom in her head." All slaves, Prince declared, "want to be free—to be free is very sweet."[85] For Prince and Sojourner, passion for the possible in this life was the bridge from oppression to liberation.

The empowering presence of the Holy Spirit (pneumatology) also pervades the narratives of this era. The Spirit empowered autonomy and independent behavior that resisted the hegemony that infringed upon slave culture. "The slave narratives testify to the presence of hope, human dignity, and self-affirmation that bear witness to the presence of God. This was the *pneumatos* (God's Spirit), a liberating presence which created and sustained the will of

---

83. Gates, ed., *Narrative of Sojourner Truth*, 164–65.
84. Ibid., 164.
85. *History of Mary Prince*, 22–23.

an enslaved people against those people and institutions that perpetrated the exploitation of African American chattel."[86]

The Spirit empowered slave women to stand in prophetic critique of the race, class, and gender oppression in their lives and community. Rather than seeing herself as the Jezebel of the community, Old Elizabeth likened herself to Mary, the mother of Jesus, who was overshadowed by the Holy Spirit. In the first paragraph of her narrative, she observed that from the age of five years old she "often felt the overshadowing of the Lord's Spirit, without at all understanding what it meant."[87] By age thirteen, she had an encounter with the Spirit that taught her to pray, "Christ save me." She immediately "felt like a new creature in Christ."[88] Though she lived in an area where she did not hear the preached word, she noted that she went in haystacks and "the presence of the Lord overshadowed me, and I was filled with sweetness and joy, and was a vessel filled with holy oil."[89] Old Elizabeth moved from a victim of abuse and violence to a vessel of God's Holy Spirit. When Elizabeth proclaimed that God had called her to preach, she was persecuted by the elders. She noted that she would hesitate "for some time as to whether or not I would take up the cross [preach] or no, I arose, and after expressing a few words, the Spirit came upon me with life. . . . I was so full I hardly knew whether I was in the body, or out of the body." The cross was a metaphor for troubles, while "the Spirit came upon me" referred to empowerment by the Holy Spirit similar to the Spirit descending upon Jesus at his baptism (John 2:32). She also likened herself to Paul, who wrote in 2 Corinthians 12:2, "whether in the body or out of the body I do not know."

When Elizabeth assembled women and preached to them, the elders were offended and attempted to silence her, but to no avail.

> At one of the meetings, a vast number of the white inhabitants of the place, and many coloured people attended—many no doubt from curiosity to hear what the old coloured woman had to say. One, a great scripturian, fixed himself behind the door with pen and ink, in order to take down the discourse in shorthand; but the Almighty Being anointed me with such a portion of his Spirit, that he cast away his paper and pen, and heard the discourse with patience, and was affected, for the Lord wrought powerful on his heart. After the meeting he came forward and offered me his hand with solemnity on his countenance, and handed me something to pay for my conveyance home.[90]

---

86. Cummings, "The Slave Narrative as a Source of Black Theological Discourse," 59.
87. *Memoir of Old Elizabeth*, 4.
88. Ibid., 7.
89. Ibid.
90. Ibid., 12, 13, 16.

Old Elizabeth did not faint with discouragement; she persevered with hope. Her determination for voice was grounded in her empowerment by the Spirit.

Harriet Jacobs also used a biblical metaphor to describe her master. The power and protection of God kept her from the ravage of Satan (the slave master). She alluded to the passage in 1 Peter 5:8, which describes the devil as a "roaring lion" who "prowls around, looking for someone to devour" to speak about her master's activity:

> For my master, whose restless, craving, vicious nature roved about day and night, seeking whom to devour, had just left me with stinging, scorching words; words that scratched ear and brain like fire.
>
> When he told me that I was made to obey his command in everything; that I was nothing but a slave, whose will must and should surrender to his, never before had my puny arm felt half so strong. The war of my life had begun; and though one of God's most powerless creatures, I resolved never to be conquered.[91]

Jacobs's power and ability to avoid her unprincipled master and jealous mistress was rooted in counter-hegemonic understanding of God, on the side of the oppressed, who is able to overcome Satan.

Slave women did not just talk about the possibilities for their lives and communities—they persued the possibilities. Their theology lived through them. The radical incarnational anthropology in the slave narratives was rooted in the presence of Jesus and the empowerment of the Spirit. Not only did the Word become flesh in Jesus, but their flesh became a living Word. These women were empowered by the conviction that they were human beings, created in the image of God. They were not chattel to be sold for profit, nor animals to be treated as beasts of burden. Nor were they sexual objects for the recreation of the master (or mistress), or procreating machines for the economy of slavery. They were fully human, rational beings, loved by the God of the "religion of Jesus," and led by the Spirit to seek justice. Slave women demanded a new humanity that rejected the status quo, unmasked the abuses of slavery, and worked toward the healing of the fractured slave community. The passion for freedom, humanity, and voice emboldened slave women to take extraordinary, radical means to achieve personal and communal liberation. The spirited women of these selected narratives used cunning, courage, and self-determination to move from victims of their context to transformative vessels of hope and life.

---

91. Jacobs, Incidents in the Life of a Slave Girl, 29, 31.

Chapter 3

Prisoners of Hope

*T*he seizing of voice that begins in female slave narratives is continued to an even greater extent during the periods of emancipation, reconstruction, and urbanization. The voices of ex-slave women remembering and recounting the ordeals of bondage and abuse is one of the salient features within the narratives of the emancipation period. The narratives of emancipated women not only voice the horrors of slavery,[1] but also reveal the social myths that undergird the continued dehumanization of the image of African American women. This image, formed in the late nineteenth and early twentieth centuries, was a part of the legacy of the sexual abuse and physical exploitation suffered by African American women in slavery. It is this distorted image that is the antecedent to the oppression of black women during emancipation.

In this chapter, I explore the sociohistorical context of emancipation and reconstruction that forms the backdrop of the narratives written during this period. I investigate the continued mythologies about black women's bodies that undergird the mistreatment of black women during this period. Then, I explore the texts themselves in detail. A womanist textual analysis of narratives of this era reveals the impact of the sociohistorical context, and stereotypical notions of black women, on narrative content and black women's religious assertions. This chapter concludes with a discussion of the focus of black women's hope during this period and the theological themes that emerge in the selected narratives.

---

1. The conversion stories of ex-slaves reveal situations of abuse and violence and speak graphically of the conversion experience and its relation to their life experiences. See Clifton Johnson, *God Struck Me Dead: Religious Conversion Experiences and Autobiographies of Ex-Slaves* (Philadelphia: Pilgrim Press, 1969).

The Sociohistorical Context of the Emancipation Era

Emancipation is the broad term used in this work to designate the periods of the emancipation, reconstruction/urbanization, from roughly 1866 through the 1950s. This term seems appropriate because the period from the end of de jure slavery through reconstruction and urbanization was a period in which black people struggled to liberate themselves from physical, psychological, economic, and social slavery. Black women during this period utilized public forums to "preach" sociopolitical freedom and cultural uplift for black women and the black community in general. Once physical slavery ended, the fight for equality and basic human rights made clear the oppression under which black people still labored.

By the late nineteenth century, the black population of the United States numbered more than four million compared to just over 700,000 in the late eighteenth century. Pre–Civil War statistics indicate that the majority of blacks (85 percent or more) were slaves. The legal end of slavery occurred in 1865 with the signing of the Emancipation Proclamation. Yet, the psychosocial, economic, and historical effects of slavery had become intrinsic to American society. The institution of slavery no longer gripped the souls and psyche of black folk, but its progeny, institutionalized racism, took its place. The social stratification that emerged during slavery in the general society, as well as in the slave community, continued to develop and mature in sophistication and impact on the lives of African American women.[2] The slave-master relationship of slavocracy was replaced with the new slavery, sharecropping. House slaves, artisans, and field slaves were replaced by mulatto elites, a growing black middle class, and lower-class service workers, respectively. While industrialization of the late nineteenth century created employment opportunities for women, African American women were still restricted primarily to low-paying domestic or service jobs.

Emancipation was not an immediate or punctilious event. Rather, emancipation was a contorted process. African Americans no longer worked as slave property for a master but began to provide for their own livelihood and economic survival.[3] Yet, for many African American women, emancipation meant continuing to work in the fields or engaging in domestic labor in white people's homes. White women who remained at home, caring for children, cleaning the house, and cooking, were working on issues of personal fulfill-

---

2. For an extensive discussion of the social stratification of the black community during the emancipation period, see Marcia Riggs, *Awake, Arise and Act: A Womanist Call for Black Liberation* (Cleveland: Pilgrim Press, 1994).

3. Emilie Townes, *Womanist Justice, Womanist Hope* (Atlanta: Scholars Press, 1993), 42.

ment as wives and mothers. White women were attempting to adhere to the tenets of the "cult of true womanhood," which elevated domesticity, submissiveness, piety, and purity. Black women who worked in the homes of white people were struggling with survival issues for themselves and their families. They were often forced to take poorly compensated jobs as washerwomen or domestics. Unlike the situation under slavocracy, however, African American women who worked in white homes usually now refused to live in their employer's home.

During the progressive era, particularly between 1890 and 1919, the number of women seeking training for professional jobs, such as nursing or social work, increased dramatically. Yet black women who were able to obtain training and professional credentials were often denied jobs. They were frequently restricted to jobs in black communities where blacks could barely (or sometimes rarely) afford to pay them. Many teachers were forced to work as domestics in order to provide for their basic needs.

A significant event of this era for black women was World War I. The war dramatically influenced the lives of poor and racially oppressed persons. The defense industry provided fairly good–paying jobs for women, but these positions were usually given to white women who were beginning to work outside the home as men went to war. The black women's club movement, which had emerged in the late nineteenth century, organized a wage earner's association in an attempt to help black working women protect their wages. The club movement was a socioreligious movement that actively critiqued race, gender, and class oppression. It was a social movement in that it provided an ethos that questioned prevailing power dynamics and ideologies. The club movement was religious in that it worked in and through the church to provide leadership training.[4] Fannie Barrier Williams, one of the founding mothers of the National Association of Colored Women, asserted in 1900 that:

> the training which first enabled colored women to organize and successfully carry on club work was originally obtained in church work. These churches have been and still are the great preparatory schools in which the primary lessons of social order, mutual trustfulness and united effort have been taught. . . . The meaning of unity of effort for the common good, the development of social sympathies grew into woman's consciousness through the privileges of church work.[5]

---

4. Marcia Riggs does an extensive study of the influence of the club movement in black women's lives in *Awake, Arise and Act*, 62–75.

5. Fannie Barrier Williams, "The Club Movement Among Colored Women of America," in *A New Negro for a New Century*, ed. Booker T. Washington, N. B. Wood, and Fannie Barrier Williams (New York: Arno Press, 1969), 383.

It was through the printing press and organizations such as the club movement that black women reasserted their voices; challenged race, class, gender oppression; and spiritually nurtured themselves and their communities to transform the victimization of the emancipation, pre–civil rights period.

Narratives During Emancipation

The narratives of emancipated women fall between 1866 and 1950. This period is a watershed of activity, including reconstruction, urbanization, and migration to the North by thousands of freed slave men and women. During emancipation, personal narratives continued to be popular in black literary tradition over other literary forms. There were several reasons for their popularity. First, narratives were political and directed propaganda toward the outside world. The narratives of slavery were political documents that argued for the full humanity of black people and against the institution of slavery. The narratives were a vehicle for espousing the "racial uplift," that is, the betterment of black society, that permeated black sociopolitical movements. During emancipation, narratives continued the quest of debunking the dehumanizing propaganda regarding black women. The focus of narratives of this period shifted from personal atrocities to public battles against stereotypical myths about black women and the oppression of black people in society in general.

Narratives provided an internal sense of order and control for persons from whom the external world demanded subservience and dependence. The self-generated and self-motivated narrative tended to unify one's point of view and shape living into coherent, meaningful patterns.[6] The narratives of emancipation helped make sense out of the unanticipated, indiscriminate, and unforeseeable occurrences in black women's lives. The narrative becomes the "sword of the spirit," the instrument of prophetic critique of the injustices and hopes of black women.

Narrative was an opportunity to blend literary convention and cultural activity so that imagination and history converged. The narratives were more than the tedious "facts" of emancipated black women's personal stories. They were an artful weaving of personal history set in creative forms to capture the interest of the reader.[7]

---

6. Pamela S. Bromberg, "The Development of Narrative Technique in Margaret Drabble's Novel," in *Journal of Narrative Techniques* 16 (1986): 179.

7. See William Andrews's discussion of imagination and personal history in *To Tell a Free Story: The First One Hundred Years of Afro-American Autobiography, 1700–1865* (Urbana: University of Illinois Press, 1986), 2–3.

Finally, narrative was a way of connecting the writer's individual story with the collective human story.[8] The narratives of emancipation engaged in a corrective historiography that included the contributions of black women to the betterment of the dominant culture, as well as to the life of the black community. In their history is woven a theology and hope that empowers black women to fight against obstacles and oppression.

The personal narrative genre of emancipation take two primary forms: the book-length, firsthand accounts of selected black women's lives during the period of 1866 through the 1950s, and the ex-slave interviews collected in the 1930s by the Work Progress Administration (WPA).[9] Black women published a significantly larger number of narratives and ex-slave interviews during this period, compared to narratives written during de jure slavery. However, many of the emancipation narratives have been lost or discarded.[10] The narratives also included voices from the border states, whereas the ex-slave interviews are predominately from Southern states.

While both narratives and interviews generally cover many of the same topics and themes, each has its own distinct advantages. Narratives have several advantages over the ex-slave interviews. First, the age of persons writing their narrative was significant. Narratives were usually written by younger persons, twenty-eight years younger than interviewees, on the average. Also, persons recording their narratives could usually recall slavery both as an adult and as a child. By the time the ex-slave interviews were gathered in the 1930s, many of the respondents were very elderly and only remembered slavery as a child. Last, the narratives tended to be book length, and thus they permit scholars to explore the writer's personal experiences, recurrent themes, and patterns.[11]

The book-length personal narratives used in this chapter are the lives of Lucy A. Delaney and Kate Drumgoold. I also return briefly to the life of

8. Nellie Y. McKay, "Nineteenth-Century Black Women's Spiritual Autobiographies: Religious Faith and Self-Empowerment" in *Interpreting Women's Lives: Feminist Theory and Personal Narratives*, ed. The Personal Narrative Group (Bloomington: Indiana University Press, 1989), 140.

9. I use the terms *narratives* and *ex-slave interviews* to differentiate between the two forms to clarify the type of emancipation narrative to which I am referring. Emancipation narrative is the inclusive term I use to designate both book-length personal narratives and the ex-slave interviews. Historians and theologians classify the ex-slave interviews as a narrative genre. See, for instance, Will Coleman, Dwight Hopkins, and George Cummings in *Cut Loose Your Stammering Tongue: Black Theology in the Slave Narratives* (Maryknoll, N.Y.: Orbis Books, 1991), and Charles T. Davis and Henry Louis Gates Jr., *The Slave's Narrative* (New York: Oxford University Press, 1985).

10. For an extensive discussion of the characteristics of narratives and ex-slave interviews, see John Blassingame, "Using the Testimony of Ex-Slaves: Approaches and Problems," in *The Slave's Narrative*, 78–94.

11. Ibid., 92.

Sojourner Truth, who lived half of her life as an emancipated woman. Sojourner's experiences bridge the movement from slavery to emancipation in the North and foreshadow emancipation in the South.

Another primary source for discerning the sociohistorical, political, and religious development of black women during emancipation is the ex-slave interviews, known as the WPA Narratives, conducted by the Federal Works Project.[12] The ex-slave interviews have the advantage over book-length narratives of giving voice to persons who probably would never have published their stories without the WPA interviews. The interviews reflect the lives of "average" black people, sought out for the express purpose of obtaining and recording their experience and recollection of slavery. The narratives were usually written by persons who had the "means," or the connections, to get them published.[13] The interviews also include a large percentage of women's stories. Whereas only 12 percent of the slave narratives written before 1865 were written by women, over 50 percent of the ex-slave interviews are interviews of women. The ex-slave interviews and the narratives of this period complement each other and provide a picture of the multitextured lives and religious beliefs of black women during emancipation, reconstruction, and urbanization. They unmask, and debunk, stereotypical notions and disclose the abuse of black women's bodies.

Because of the brevity of the ex-slave interviews, which tend to be two or three pages long, it will be necessary to use several. The stories, experiences, and religious expressions in the ex-slave interviews are consistent with the book-length narratives and the literature of slavery. Ex-slave interviews referenced in this chapter are Priscilla Albright of Georgia, Margaret Nickerson of Florida, Phyllis Green of South Carolina, Mary Gladdy and Martha Spence Burton of Texas, Fannie Moore of North Carolina, Annie Young of Oklahoma, and Clara Brim of Louisiana.

But before turning to the narratives of emancipation, it is necessary to consider the mythology that undergirds their content. Just as the prevailing social mythologies regarding black women influenced the content of slave narratives, emancipation and contemporary narratives are influenced by their own particular presuppositions and myths about black women.

---

12. Most of the ex-slave interviews noted in this chapter are taken from George Rawick's forty-volume, indexed collection. George Rawick, ed., *The American Slave: A Composite Autobiography*, 18 vols. (Westport, Conn.: Greenwood Press, 1972) and George Rawick, ed., *The American Slave: A Composite Autobiography*, supplement, series I, 12 vols. (Westport, Conn.: Greenwood Press, 1977).

13. Ibid., 84.

The Disfigured Image of Black Women

The dehumanization of legal slavery ended with emancipation, but the sexual exploitation of black women in the North and the South did not. Emancipation was an era of crude stereotypes in which African American women's sexuality was represented negatively in popular, as well as academic, discourse. Regardless of their income, education, or occupation, African American women were the embodiment of deviance, a disfigured image.

All black women were characterized as sluts. A 1904 newspaper quotes a white woman as saying:

> Negro women evidence more nearly the popular idea of the total depravity than the men. . . . When a man's mother, wife and daughters are all immoral women, there is little room in his fallen nature for the aspiration of honor or virtue. . . . I cannot image such a creation as a virtuous black woman.[14]

Because of these stereotypical notions of innate promiscuity, African American women who were raped had no legal redress. Courts did not convict white men who raped black females beyond the age of puberty simply because of the presumed promiscuity of black women.[15]

The victimization of black women during the emancipation era was under-girded by the stereotypical notions of women that developed during slavery. White women were "good wives," or ladies, but African American women were "Negro wenches," Jezebels, Mammy, and "bad black women." That which characterized white women in the seventeenth, eighteenth, and nineteenth centuries as "good wives" characterized nineteenth- and early-twentieth-century black women as "Negro wenches." The good wife was a (white) woman who kept her house clean, cared for her children, was subservient to her husband, and was sexually available. Black women were forced to keep the master's house clean and care for the master's children, objectified as less than human, and violated at the caprice of master and mistress. Though black women filled the same roles of "good wives," they were characterized as "Negro wenches."[16]

---

14. "Experiences of the Race Problem by a Southern White Woman," as quoted in Evelyn Higginbotham, *Righteous Discontent: The Women's Movement in the Black Baptist Church, 1880–1920* (Cambridge, Mass.: Harvard University Press, 1993), 190.

15. Higginbotham, *Righteous Discontent*, 190.

16. Alexander B. Groshart, ed., *The Poems and Literary Prose of Alexander Wilson*, 2 vols. (Paisley, Scotland: Alex Gardner, 1876), 1: 167–68 as cited in Deborah Gray White, *Ar'n't I a Woman? Female Slaves in the Plantation South* (New York: W. W. Norton, 1985), 30.

The Jezebel mythology, which emerged during slavery, continued and depicted black women as lewd and lascivious beings (not necessarily human beings) governed by an insatiable libido, who solicited sexual advances from white men. The Mammy myth resurfaced as *Aunt Jemima*, a fat, asexual, innocuous, mother figure who was portrayed as "caring for the children, performing and supervising household chores, lending an ear and offering advice to the master, mistress, and white children."[17] Aunt Jemima symbolized the "cultural uplift" of black people, and at the same time was a sainted representation of Southern notions of domesticity and motherhood.[18] The Mammy/Aunt Jemima mythology pervaded movies, pancake boxes, and syrup bottles and was imprinted in the psyche of American society.

The Jezebel-Mammy images of emancipation rationalized and legitimized the mistreatment of black women.[19] The prevailing sexualized mythologies regarding black women were juxtaposed with notions of blacks as cannibals. These myths were "supported" among "scholars" by "scientific" evidence in the form of social Darwinism. Social Darwinism was a racially denigrating theory that ranked human beings. Blacks (or anyone with non-Anglo-Saxon features) were depicted as less than human, tending to "love idleness and orgies, evil for its own sake, and desired not only to murder but to 'mutilate the corpse, tear its flesh, and drink its blood.'"[20] The scientific support of social Darwinism moved the image of blacks from passive, docile children to dangerous, lustful savages. These mythologies pervaded late-nineteenth- and early-twentieth-century notions of black women. By the early and mid-twentieth centuries, these myths had been re-depicted as the "bad black woman" (and "the black rapist" for black men).

The "bad black woman" was bad in the sense of loose and hypersexual, and thus did not deserve the respect and consideration of white women.[21] These myths were reinforced in several ways. Intermarriage was illegal; black

---

17. Ibid., 59.

18. *Cultural uplift* refers to social activism as well as philanthropic activities by black people during emancipation/reconstruction/urbanization to seek human rights, jobs, education, or training that improved the position and perception of black people in American society. See Gerda Lerner, *Black Women in White America: A Documentary History* (New York: Vintage Books, 1972), 437–77.

19. "The Jezebel image excused miscegenation, the sexual exploitation of black women, and the mulatto population. It could not, however, calm Southern fears of moral slippage and 'mongrelization,' or man's fear of woman's emasculating sexual powers. But the Mammy could. Mammy helped endorse the service of black women in Southern households, as well as the close contact between whites and blacks that such service demanded. Together Jezebel and Mammy did a lot of explaining and soothed many a troubled conscience." White, *Ar'n't I a Woman?*, 61.

20. Paula Giddings, *When and Where I Enter: The Impact of Black Women on Race and Sex in America* (New York: W. Morrow, 1984), 79.

21. Gerda Lerner, *The Majority Finds Its Past: Placing Women in American History* (New York: Vintage Books, 1992), 163. For a discussion of this topic, see 163–71.

women were never addressed as Miss or Mrs.; black women could not try on clothes in department stores; black women and black men were often provided a single toilet facility; there were taboos against blacks and whites mixing in social settings; and there were different legal sanctions for rape or molestation of black women and white women.[22] With the changing context and its legitimizing mythologies came new challenges to the lives of black women. Sojourner Truth also exemplifies this.

A "Representative" Black Woman

The life of Sojourner Truth bridges slavery and the emancipation period. Sojourner was born in the late 1790s and lived until 1883. She lived approximately half of her life in slavery in New York, which became a "free state" on July 4, 1827, and the other half she lived as an emancipated woman. We looked at her life as she exemplified the struggles for humanity and freedom characteristic of slavery. Her life after emancipation typifies black women's quest for voice, autonomy, and equality that characterized the emancipation period. As historian Nell Painter notes, in many ways Sojourner was "a representative African-American woman" of these two periods. Truth was representative of the struggles of the period as well as the hopes and spiritual resources.[23]

Sojourner traveled the country seizing opportunities to speak, even when part of the crowd preferred she remain silent. Her voice was a public one lifted to engage the battle for the equality of black women and blacks in general. Frances Gage recorded that preceding Sojourner's famous "Ain't I a Woman" speech in Akron, Ohio, several persons in the crowd shouted, "Don't let her speak. Don't let her speak." Sojourner was determined to respond to the claim that men had superior rights and privileges over women. A male minister in the crowd declared, "[i]f God had desired the equality of women, he would have given them some token of his will through the birth, life, and death of our Savior."[24] Sojourner made her way to the front, and with the crowd in an

---

22. Ibid., 163–64.

23. Painter notes "Isabella discovered the secret power that black women have tapped into over the generations to counter the negation they experience in the world. In sanctification they have located a power that has made possible survival and autonomous action when all their means fail. More than anything else she did or said in her life, this ability to act with the support of a powerful supernatural force and to mine extraordinary resources made Sojourner Truth a representative African American woman." Nell Painter, *Sojourner Truth: A Life, a Symbol* (New York: W. W. Norton, 1996), 30–31.

24. Henry Louis Gates Jr., ed., *Narratives of Sojourner Truth: A Bondswoman of Olden Time, with a History of Her Labors and Correspondence Drawn from Her "Book of Life"* (New York: Oxford University Press, 1991), 132–33.

uproar, rose to speak. "The tumult subsided at once, and every eye was fixed on this almost Amazon form, which stood nearly six foot high, head erect, and eye piercing the upper air, like one in a dream. At her first word there was a profound hush."[25] Sojourner captivated the audience and delivered her speech.

Sojourner was well known by friends, supporters, and those who opposed her person and her platform. In Sojourner's *Book of Life*, she recorded a meeting with President Abraham Lincoln to thank him for his role in freeing the slaves. She thanked President Lincoln for being an instrument of God to emancipate her people. She admitted to the president that she had never heard of him before he ran for president. He smiled at her and replied, "I had heard of you many times before that."[26] As well known and as highly respected as she was by many, a newspaper from New Jersey made derogatory, stereotypical remarks about her. The paper reported that a church in Springfield, Union County, New Jersey was

> honored on Wednesday night by the presence of that lively old negro mummy [*sic*], whose age ranges among the hundreds—Sojourner Truth— who fifty years ago was considered a crazy woman. When respectable churches consent to admit to the houses open for worship of God every wandering negro minstrel or street spouter who profess to have a peculiar religious experience, or some grievance to redress, they render themselves justly liable to public ridicule. . . . She is a crazy, ignorant, repelling negress, and her guardians would do a Christian act to restrict her to private life.[27]

Sojourner was not deterred from her mission by such defamation of character. While sexual abuse of Sojourner is no longer mentioned in her *Book of Life*, the questioning of whether or not she was a woman was just as dehumanizing. Although Nell Painter challenges the validity of the story, Frances Gage recorded that Sojourner bared her breasts to prove that she was indeed a woman.[28] Sojourner continued to walk proudly "with the air of a queen" and to fight for the right to speak to the oppression of women and blacks in general. This kind of attack in public, in the newspaper, books, and movies was characteristic of the abuse of black women during the emancipation period. Though slavery had ended, the sexual and physical oppression of black women continued. Many slaves left the plantations and migrated north for

---

25. Ibid., 133.
26. Ibid., 178.
27. Ibid., 203–4.
28. Painter discusses extensively the exploitation of Sojourner Truth's life by Gage (and others) for the purpose of creating a cultural symbol. See Painter's *Sojourner Truth: A Life, a Symbol.*

work and opportunities; however, many were forced to remain on plantations. Whether on the Southern plantation or in the North doing domestic work, black women still had to struggle with sexual and physical exploitation, which was undergirded by disfigured images of black women.

The Changing Context
and the Struggles of Freed Black Women

The shifting structure of the personal narrative genre by black women elucidates the impact of the sociohistorical context on the lives of black women. By the late nineteenth and early twentieth centuries, many black female autobiographical narratives dealt less with the personal atrocities of slavery and more with the public quest for autonomy, equality, and voice.[29] The structure of the genre moved from the typical structure of the slave narrative to a narrative structure that was nonsequential, topical, and less personal.[30] By the early twentieth century, most of the persons who held the treasury of knowledge regarding slavery were becoming advanced in years and many had already died. Historians, scholars, and the government undertook a vast project to collect information about slavery from emancipated persons through the Federal Writers Project so that the experiences, values, and hopes of enslaved persons would not be lost forever. Through this federal project, thousands of ex-slaves were interviewed and their stories preserved. The ex-slave interviews show the struggles and hopes of ex-slaves from the vantage of freed individuals whose voice did not have an abolitionist intent.

Perhaps more than any other narratives, the ex-slave interviews clearly demonstrate the impact of the sociohistorical context on the lives of black

---

29. Some of the more prominent black female narratives of this period are those of Maria Stewart (1803–1879), Ida B. Wells (1862–1931), and Anna Julia Cooper (1858–1964). I have included Stewart here because she wrote as a free black woman in the antebellum North. Though free, she did experience physical violence because of her outspokenness against the oppression of women and blacks, which she described in many published articles and newspapers. The narratives of these women typify the less personal narratives of emancipation that deviated from the structure of the slave narratives and had the express purpose of seizing voice, autonomy, and equality. See Maria Stewart, *Productions of Mrs. Maria Stewart* (Boston: Friends of Freedom and Virtue, 1835); repr., ed. Henry Louis Gates Jr. (New York: Oxford University Press, 1988); Anna Julia Cooper, *A Voice from the South by a Black Woman of the South* (Ohio: The Aldine Printing House, 1892); repr., ed. Henry Louis Gates Jr. (New York: Oxford University Press, 1988); Alfreda Duster, ed., *Crusade for Justice: The Autobiography of Ida B. Wells* (Chicago: University of Chicago Press, 1970).

30. Slave narratives tended to take a prescribed pattern of sequential nature. "I was born . . . , my parents were . . . , the recounting of abuses, and the quest for freedom." See James Olney's extensive discussion of the literary structure of autobiographical slave narrative, " 'I Was Born': Slave Narratives, Their Status as Autobiography and as Literature," in Davis and Gates, eds., *The Slave's Narrative*.

women and the content of their narratives. It is imperative that one discusses the continuity between slavery and freedom in order to understand American racism and, I would add, sexism. The fact that many slaves were forced to remain on the same plantations after slavery is vital to comprehending the continued victimization of black women and blacks in general in this country.[31]

While freedom, autonomy, and equality were the quest of black women, they had not been prepared economically, emotionally, socially, or educationally for them. Even slaves who escaped soon discovered that freedom, without equal access to opportunities, work, and resources, was a hollow victory and left them victims to another type of oppression. Priscilla Albright, an ex-slave born in Georgia in 1853, made this fact poignantly clear in her interview recorded in August of 1936. She noted:

> Until within the past few years, this good old woman worked hard from the "first day of freedom." At the first blush of freedom . . . the Negroes were staggered. They did not know what to do. Then their joys knew no bounds; they went wild. The very thought that they were free overwhelmed them. Some had hysterics, some shouted, some prayed and some sang, and many took to the highways and the byways, just to exercise their independence, and walked and roamed, aimless, for days! Finally, however, there came a reaction: the Negro was on his own. He no longer had a white man to look to for his daily bread, his clothes, medical attention when needed, and a free shelter to lay his head. The transition demoralized many Negroes, particularly those of the younger generation.[32]

Sexual abuse and violence toward black women did not end with emancipation. Annie Young related in her interview:

> My auntie's old Master tried to have her and she run off out in de woods and when he put those blood hounds or nigger hounds on her trail he catched her and hit her in de head wid something like de stick de police carry, and he knocked a hole in her head and she bleed like a stuck hog, and he made her have him. She told her mistress, and mistress told her to go ahead 'cause

---

31. George Rawick notes, "I am struck, moreover, by the fact that many ex-slaves clearly did not distinguish between the experience under slavery and that after abolition. The plantation system did not change drastically for most ex-slaves after the end of slavery, and many continued to live and work on the same plantation where they had formerly been slaves. Indeed when interviewed in the 1930s some were still living on the same plantation they worked. I believe evidence of this important continuity between slavery and freedom must be made available if we are to understand the depths of the system of American racism [and sexism]." George Rawick, *The American Slave: A Composite Autobiography*, vol. 1: "From Sundown to Sunup: The Making of the Black Community" (Westport, Conn.: Greenwood Publishing Co., 1972), xviii.

32. Priscilla Albright, quoted in Rawick, *The American Slave*, vol. 12, 2.

he's gonna kill you. And he had dem two women and she had some chillun nearly white, and master and dey all worked in de fields side by side.[33]

For many slaves the violence after emancipation also grew worse instead of better. Fannie Moore noted in her interview:

> After de war, de Ku Klux broke out. Oh miss, dey war mean. . . . Dey keep close watch on dem (black folk). . . . Dey nebber go 'roun' much in de day. Jes night. Dey take de pore niggers away in de woods an' beat 'em an' hang 'em. . . . We lib on de same plantation 'till de chillun all grown an' mammy an' pappy both die. Den we leave.[34]

Abuse and violence were no longer restricted to the master-slave relationship but was perpetrated in organized, socially sanctioned, public groups such as the KKK. Thus, as I noted earlier in this chapter, *a characteristic of the narratives of emancipation was that they gave public voice against the oppression and stereotypical notions regarding women and blacks.*

A second characteristic of the narratives of this era was to provide internal order (personal and communal) in an externally chaotic unpredictable world. One way order was sought was through the quest for autonomy. Lucy Delaney's narrative, *From the Darkness Cometh the Light or Struggle for Freedom*, typifies this feature. Her narrative was published in 1891 in St. Louis, Missouri. The title of the narrative captures Lucy's journey from the unpredictable life of slavery toward a more ordered existence in emancipation. Her narrative begins with the dark details of enslavement and traces her movement from subservience and dependence to independence and autonomy.

Lucy was born into slavery. As a child, her mother had been kidnapped, gagged, and bound in Illinois and sold into slavery. Lucy's childhood was free from the abuses of slavery, but after the death of the family's first master, her family was separated. Her father was "sold South" away from the family. This was the beginning of her quest for freedom and the answer to the lingering question of how long a righteous God would permit such abuse. Lucy lamented "[s]lavery! Cursed slavery! What crimes has it invoked! And oh! What retribution has a righteous God visited upon these traders in human flesh?! . . . Oh! Lord, how long, how long?"[35] Lucy also witnessed the auction of her mother

---

33. Annie Young, quoted in *The WPA Oklahoma Slave Narratives*, ed. T. Lindsay Baker and Julia Baker (Norman: University of Oklahoma Press, 1996), 506.

34. Fannie Moore, quoted in Rawick, *The American Slave*, vol. 15, 39.

35. Lucy A. Delaney, *From Darkness Cometh the Light or Struggle for Freedom* (St. Louis: Publishing House of J. T. Smith, 1891); repr. in *Six Women's Slave Narratives*, ed. Henry Louis Gates Jr. (New York: Oxford University Press, 1988), 14–15.

to the highest bidder, for five hundred and fifty dollars. Her mother escaped three weeks later. When informed of her mother's escape, Lucy's retort was a cry that can still be heard almost every Sunday in the black church: "God is good." Her mother was captured in Chicago but was returned to St. Louis by "the negro-catchers" under the Fugitive Slave law which made it illegal to aid (for example, even to offer a glass of water) or protect runaway slaves. But times were different now. Lucy's mother retained a lawyer and sued for her freedom. She was able to prove that she had been born free, kidnapped, and sold into slavery. The jury upheld her freedom. However, while this process was going on, Lucy was still in slavery. Her mistress was teaching her how to work, since she had never been enslaved and required to do work, such as the weekly washing and ironing. Lucy washed the mistress's clothes in the muddy waters of the Mississippi River. The clothes were discolored and ruined, and her mistress verbally abused her, saying, "Lucy, you do not want to work, you are a lazy, good for nothing nigger!"[36] Lucy records her quest for autonomy and voice. She noted, "I was angry at being called a nigger and replied, 'you don't know nothing, yourself, about it, and you expect a poor ignorant girl to know more than you do yourself; if you had any feeling you would get somebody to teach me, and then I'd do well enough.' "[37] When her mistress then threatened to whip her, Lucy defiantly said to her, "You have no business to whip me. I don't belong to you."[38] Lucy added that her mother had taught her that she was a free woman and should not die as a slave. Lucy had "a strong feeling of independence which would invariably crop out in these encounters with [her] mistress; and when [Lucy] thus spoke, saucily, I must confess, she [her mistress] opened her eyes in angry amazement. . . ."[39]

Lucy was as determined not to be whipped as her mistress was determined to whip her. Lucy's determination went beyond verbal response to physical disarmament of her mistress. "I rebelled against such government, and would not permit her to strike me; she used shovel, tongs and broom stick in vain, as I disarmed her as fast as she picked up each weapon."[40] Lucy refused to be subservient and dependent and fought for independence, equality, and autonomy.

The battles in this era for freedom, autonomy, and voice involved the individual, God, and the legal system. Lucy's mother eventually sued for Lucy's freedom. Since Lucy had been born to a free woman, she argued, Lucy was

---

36. Ibid., 25.
37. Ibid.
38. Ibid., 26.
39. Ibid.
40. Ibid., 27.

free also. Lucy's mother "girded up her loins for the fight, and knowing that she was right, was resolved, by the help of God and a good lawyer, to win my [Lucy's] case against all opposition."[41] As Lucy listened to the closing argument by her attorney for her freedom and right to autonomy, she was invigorated. He argued that it was a violation of God's law and man's law to suggest that a free woman could give birth to a slave. "I listened with renewed hope. I felt the black storm clouds of doubt and despair were fading away, and that I was drifting into the safe harbor of the realms of truth."[42] Though Lucy spent seventeen months in jail awaiting her trial and verdict, she eventually won her freedom. As the title of her narrative suggests, Lucy's struggle for freedom was a movement from the darkness and abuses of slavery to the light of emancipation for herself and her family. She dedicated her narrative to "those who by their valor have made their name immortal."[43] Lucy utilized the resources available to her to seize her autonomy, and then recorded her experiences to ensure that her voice would be heard for generations to come. Though her victory was a personal achievement, she understood it to be significant for the black community. She concluded her narrative with the question that pervaded the emancipation period: "Can the Negro race succeed, proportionally, as well as the whites, if given the same chance and an equal start?" Lucy's question encapsulates the demand for voice and equality, free from sexual abuse and violence for black women, found in the narratives of emancipation.

Kate Drumgoold published her autobiography in 1898 in Brooklyn, New York. Though she entitled her narrative *A Slave Girl's Story*, she made it very clear in the first few pages of her narrative that she was not writing to reveal the atrocities of slavery. Rather, she wrote "for the good of those who have written and prayed that the slaves might be a free people, and have schools and books and learn to read and write for themselves."[44] For Kate, freedom equaled access to education. She noted that the newspaper revealed that black people in the South were being killed for seeking education. She was prepared and willing to die for the right of all black people to be educated. Ex-slave Margaret Nickerson recalled in her interview that the master "never 'lowed us [slaves] to have a piece of paper in our hands."[45] But with emancipation, slaves who had secretly tried to learn to read and write were able to go to school. Martha Spence Burton recalled, "after freedom pappy sent us to de

41. Ibid., 35.

42. Ibid., 41.

43. Ibid., from the dedication in the front of her narrative.

44. Kate Drumgoold, "A Slave Girl's Story" (Brooklyn, 1898); repr. in *Six Women's Slave Narratives*, 3.

45. Margaret Nickerson; quoted in Rawick, *The American Slave*, vol. 17, 1.

white teacher, and dat's why I can read and write."[46] Kate wrote with the express purpose of advancing the education of black women in an interesting and informative way.

Kate's intended purpose characterizes a third feature of emancipation narratives. *She brings the struggles of her culture to literature and intertwines them into a creative form to interest her readers and support her cause.* Her passion is expressed through her aggressiveness to celebrate freedom, and to voice the quest of black people for the educational access that whites took for granted. The violence and sexual abuse in her narrative are overshadowed by her quest to educate her people.

Kate was one of seventeen girls and one boy born to her slave parents near Petersburg, Virginia. She was a young child during the Civil War and did not experience being a slave as a teenager or adult. She referred to her mistress as her "white mother" who was "so kind to [her] dear mother and all the negros of the place."[47] She did remember her mother being sold away from the family at the beginning of the war in Richmond, Virginia. Her mother was sold to raise money so that a rich white man could pay a poor white man to take his place in the war. In addition to the monetary payment, if the poor white man survived the battle, he was to "receive a negro" after the war as additional payment. Kate does allude to very severe trials in her life that forced her to rely only on the Lord. She noted that "God had been a father and a loving mother and all else to me, and sometimes there has been enough trials in this life to make me almost forget that I had this strong arm to save me from these trials."[48] But her determination to work hard, support herself, and seize the opportunities of this new era undergirded her quest for education.

Hard work and persistent study were the keys to autonomy, equality, and voice for freed blacks, Kate asserted. In 1865 she moved to Brooklyn and worked as a domestic to save money to attend school in order to become a teacher and assist other blacks to progress educationally. Despite experiencing sickness, poverty, and exploitation, she obtained an education. Kate recalls working the whole summer, doing without necessities to save money for school only to have the money stolen from her. She borrowed money for school that year. By 1886 she had finished boarding school and four years at Wayland Seminary in Washington, D.C., and embarked on her teaching career. Though plagued by typhoid fever and frequent illness, Kate worked

---

46. Martha Spence Burton; quoted in Rawick, *The American Slave*, vol. 4, 2.
47. Ibid., 4.
48. Ibid., 30.

tirelessly in the church and the community, teaching her race so that they could gain equal access to life as free Americans.

The final characteristic of narratives of emancipation was *that they merged the individual stories with the collective human story.* Kate Drumgoold noted the interconnection between the biotext of slave women and history. She asserted, "[N]o subject can surely be more delightful than the history of a slave girl, and the many things that are linked to this life that man may search and research in the ages to come."[49] Lucy Delaney wrote but a few of the incidents of her life because she understood that history would tell the trials and triumphs of slavery. "I have brought you with me face to face with but only a few of the painful fates engendered by slavery, and the rest can be drawn from history," she asserted. Lucy followed this declaration with a list of the organizations in which she was a member, all for the express purpose of advancing the collective life of black women:

> I became a member of the Methodist Church in 1855; was elected President of the first colored society, called the "Female Union," which was the first organized exclusively for women, was elected President of a society known as the "Daughters of Zion"; was matron of "Siloam Court," No. 2, three years in succession; was the Most Ancient Matron of the "Grand Court of Missouri," . . . I am at present Past Grand Chief Preceptress of the "Daughters of Tabernacle and Knights of Tabor," and also was Secretary, and still a member of Col. Shaw Women's Relief Corps. . . . Considering the limited advantage offered to me, I have made the best use of my time, and what few talents the Lord has bestowed on me I have not "hidden in a napkin," but used them for His glory and to benefit those for whom I live. And what better can we do than to live for others![50]

Out of their involvement in the church and various socioreligious clubs, black women, like Lucy Delaney and Kate Drumgoold, sought creative ways to overcome personal struggles and to work for communal advancement. The experiences, involvements, and achievements of these women were for the cultural uplift and betterment of black women. In the midst of personal struggles (Holler) and individual triumphs (Hope) emerged the collective quest for equality, autonomy, and voice. Black women were determined to "awake, awake and arise," throw off the vestiges of slavery, and become shackled to Hope.

---

49. Drumgoold, "A Slave Girl's Story," 24.
50. Delaney, *From Darkness Cometh the Light,* 62–63.

"Prisoners of Hope": Emancipated Black Women

The narrative of Maria Stewart illuminates a function of hope in the lives of abused emancipated women. Stewart's narrative was originally published during slavery (1835), and it was expanded and republished during emancipation (1879). Stewart did not endure the abuses of slavery, because she was a free black woman. She wrote as a free black woman in the North who had a desire to transform the oppression of her people.[51] Stewart, born free in Hartford, Connecticut, in 1803, was orphaned at age five and "bound out" to work thereafter. Stewart lectured and wrote extensively during her young adult life. She spoke before "promiscuous" audiences, that is, men and women, black and white, and was "the first American-born woman to give public speeches and leave extant texts of her addresses."[52] Her public career in the black community was short-lived because she was "resented for her religious exhortations and even more for her audacity as a woman."[53] She later moved to New York and began publishing her extensive volume of letters and speeches in 1879. Stewart's work became a foundation of black women's activism for many generations to come. Her ideals reflect the Victorian ethic as well as the sharp criticism of its biases. While Stewart supported the "cult of true women's" notion that women had strong influence on the morals of their family, she adamantly resisted the notion that black women were responsible for their own degradation. She challenged black women to:

> Awake! awake! arise! No longer sleep nor slumber, but distinguish yourselves. Show forth to the world that you are endowed with noble and exalted faculties. O ye, daughters of Africa! What have ye done to immortalize your names beyond the grave? What examples have ye set before the rising generation? What foundation have ye set for the generation yet unborn?[54]

Stewart "rallied against the racism toward blacks that fueled discrimination in the North and provided the rationale for slavery in the South."[55] Hope propelled her to social, political, and religious activity. She noted, "I cannot help but exclaim, glory to God that I am yet a prisoner of hope. I rejoice that I have been found a rational and accountable creature, and that I was born to

---

51. See Stewart, *Productions of Mrs. Maria Stewart*.
52. Giddings, *When and Where I Enter*, 50.
53. Ruth Bogin and Bert James Loewenberg, eds., *Black Women in the Nineteenth-Century American Life: Their Words, Their Thoughts, Their Feelings* (University Park: Pennsylvania State University Press, 1976), 184.
54. Stewart, "Productions of Mrs. Maria Stewart," 6.
55. Giddings, *When and Where I Enter*, 50.

be born again."[56] Hope enabled her to fight against the sexual dehumanization of African American women and to fight for freedom (sociopolitical) and
voice for all. Thus, hope empowered her to move from being a victim of her
context to being a vessel of life for herself and community. Stewart's hope
characterized the passion of black women across the generations.

Hope was black women's passion for the possible in this life, as well as
secondarily, in the life to come. Their hope was the mirror image of the suffering of black people. That is, just as abuse has been maldistributed, enormous, and transgenerational, so has black women's hope. The maldistributed,
enormous, and transgenerational character of oppression of black women's
bodies has been demonstrated in the emancipation narratives and ex-slave
interviews, just as it was in the narratives written during slavery. The fact that
emancipation narratives and ex-slave interviews number over two thousand
and contain the recurrent themes of abuse and violence against black women
and their families attest to this. Sojourner's womanhood was questioned.
Lucy Delaney's "sweet" childhood erupted into violence and abuse. She saw
her mother, born free, sold away from her family. Kate Drumgoold's trials of
life were so severe that she could look to none but God to deliver her. Yet
their narratives also illuminate a passion for voice, autonomy, and equality
that was maldistributed, enormous, and transgenerational. The passion for the
possible was maldistributed, found in great proportions in black women's
emancipation narratives, as they sought to counter the multidimensional
abuse of black women during this period. Lucy Delaney noted that "[her]
pathway was thorny enough, and though there may be no roses without
thorns, [she] had thorns in plenty with no roses."[57] Her thorns without roses
did not deter her from being involved in several social organizations for the
cultural uplift of black women. Rather, I would argue, she believed the
answer to her own question—"Can the Negro race succeed proportionally as
well as whites, if given the same chance and equal start?"—was a resounding "yes," and she worked to advance her conviction. Kate Drumgoold noted
that many doors had been closed to the black race in the quest to obtain education, but she wrote and fought fervently for this right. The fact that she
could write "[T]here are many who have lost their lives in the far South in
trying to get an education, but there are many that have done well, and we
feel like giving God all the praise"[58] attests to her passion for the possible in
her life as well as her community.

---

56. Stewart, *Productions of Mrs. Maria Stewart*, 28.
57. Delany, *From Darkness Cometh the Light*, 16.
58. Drumgoold, "A Slave Girl's Story," 4.

The enormity of black women's hope is demonstrated in their life-affirming quest to actualize black women's potential and abilities in an oppressive culture. Sojourner's activism on behalf of black women's rights, Maria Stewart's political activism for black women, and Kate Drumgoold's passion for education are a few of the life-giving vehicles of emancipation. Lucy Delaney alluded to a new day dawning for black women, and blacks in general. She ended her narrative with a poem that reveals the hope for this life. The poem not only predicated a theological shift in the dominant culture but also the passion for right, and rights. She alluded to the dominant culture "learning the new Gospel"!

> The hours are growing shorter for the millions who are toiling;
> And the homes are growing better for the millions yet to be;
> And we all shall learn the lesson, how that waste and sin are spoiling
> The fairest and the finest of grand humanity.
> It is coming! It is coming! And men's thoughts are growing deeper;
> They are giving of their millions as they never gave before;
> They are learning the new Gospel, man must be his brother's keeper,
> And right, not might, shall triumph, and the selfish rule no more.[59]

This untitled poem bespeaks the hope and potential of black women given an "equal start and same chance" as whites.

As in the slave narratives, the transgenerational character of hope is evident in emancipation narratives in the recurrence of mothers, aunts, and daughters instilling hope and determination in each other and their children through their faith in God, each other, and community. Kate's mother instilled in her and her siblings the love and passion for freedom. Kate recorded "all of my mother's children were like herself in their love of freedom. My mother was one the master could not do anything to make her feel like a slave and she would battle with them to the last that she would not recognize them as lord and master and she was right."[60] Kate had a multigenerational goal in that she labored "for the good of the race, that their children might be bright and shining lights."[61]

Ex-slave Priscilla Albright also talked about the transgenerational realization of hope. Her Aunt Cilia's life is a "summary of the immediate after effects of freedom upon the people of her race." Her aunt "reared a family of ten children [and] labored in the fields. Her husband was a farmer; however, at one time he was in the U.S. Army. And, thanks to the government, his widow now

---

59. Delaney, *From Darkness Cometh the Light*, 64.
60. Drumgoold, "A Slave Girl's Story," 32.
61. Ibid., 3.

draws a pension of $30.00 a month. She also owns her own home and is comfortable in her old age, enjoying a comfort that she richly deserves."[62]

Transgenerational hope is evident in the narratives immediately following emancipation as well as in the ex-slave interviews recorded in the 1930s. This hope was primarily a this-worldly goal, as in the slave narratives. Though the object of hope changed to some degree from slavery to emancipation, black women were primarily concerned with obtaining a better condition of existence for themselves and their community in this world. Once physical freedom was obtained, psychological and economical freedom, autonomy, and equality became the objects of their hope.

The metaphorical use of biblical language that interweaved the slave narratives is also evident in the selected narratives of emancipation. Women's rights advocate and abolitionist Sojourner Truth likened herself to biblical Queen Esther. Esther became queen after Vashti, the queen who dared challenge the patriarchal objectification of women and refused to disrobe herself for King Ahasuerus and his comrades. Vashti's refusal to expose herself not only defied the king but threatened to empower other women to refuse to be objectified. (See Esther 1.)[63] So Vashti was dethroned. Esther dared to speak to the king without being summoned to his presence. She risked her life to speak on behalf of her people. Sojourner refused to be silenced regarding the oppression of women. Even when the crowd cried, "Don't let her speak," Sojourner must have resolved, like Esther, "I will go to the king, though it is against the law; and if I perish, I perish" (Esther 4:16). Sojourner knew that if she kept "silent at such a time as this, relief and deliverance would rise for the Jews (her people—blacks and women) from another quarter" (Esther 4:14, my trans.). Sojourner's response was "I do not want any man to be killed, but I am sorry to see them so short minded. But we will have our rights; see if we don't; and you can't stop us from them; see if you can. You may hiss as much as you like, but it is comin'."[64]

Kate Drumgoold used the Exodus deliverance motif that was so prevalent in the slave narratives. She surmised that God delivered black people in the same way God delivered the children of Israel. She wrote:

62. Albright, quoted in Rawick, *The American Slave*, vol. 12, 2.

63. Nell Painter challenges the validity of the breast-baring incident by Truth as a literary device by Frances Gage to immortalize the image or symbol of Sojourner's life. Given Sojourner's tendency to align herself closely with the book of Esther, I would argue that Painter is correct: that Sojourner would not have bared her breast. She would have refused to disrobe like Queen Vashti. See Painter, *Sojourner Truth: A Life, a Symbol*, 138–42, 171, 220, 264, 266–68, 272.

64. Elizabeth Cady Stanton, Susan B. Anthony, and Matilda Joslyn Gage, eds., *History of Woman Suffrage*, vol. 1 (New York: Fowler & Wells, 1881), 568 as cited by Nell Painter, *Sojourner Truth: A Life, a Symbol*, 136.

... and the Lord, in His love for us and to us as a race, has ever found favor in His sight, for when we were in the land of bondage [slavery] He heard the prayers of the faithful ones, and came to deliver them out of the land of Egypt. For God loves those that are oppressed, and will save them when they cry unto Him, and when they put their trust in Him.[65]

Not only was God a deliverer of the oppressed, but Kate noted that God was the empowered of abused. The Lord preached the word through her, "a feeble one of the dust, and what cannot the Lord help us to do if only we trust in Him and if we strive to live for His honor and glory on this side of the Jordan?" God impassioned her on this side of Jordan to fight for voice, autonomy, and equality denied all blacks, but especially women.

Lucy Delaney used a biblical metaphor drawn from Ephesians 5 to describe her mother's battle for Lucy's freedom. Lucy's mother put on the full armor of God and then stood firmly for her belief that her only crime was wanting that which was her birthright—freedom. Her mother "girded up her loins for the fight, and knowing that she was right, was resolved, by the help of God and a good lawyer, to win my case against all opposition."[66] Though she referenced the Bible, she made clear that human activism was a necessary component of getting her freedom. Her religion was not a passive religion, nor an opiate that enabled her to acquiesce to her circumstances; rather, it enabled her to stand with determined resolve.

Ex-slave Phyllis Green related the use of a biblical metaphor that was commonly used by whites and taught to blacks, to explain the "curse" of being black. Phyllis's mistress caught her laughing to herself one morning in the kitchen, and Phyllis related this story:

When I came to wuk dis morning I pass a colored man, 'e was dat drunk I bus out laughing right off an' 'e say, "Phyllis, don't you laugh at no drunk man, aint yu know dat what made you black, cause Ham 'e laugh at 'e pa when 'e was drunk an' 'e cuss 'em. Dat why we is black today."[67]

In spite of being black and female, like Lucy and Kate, Phyllis did not acquiesce to the oppressive religious ideologies. When asked by her mistress if slaves were not better off in this country because they could be "taught religion and better ways of living," Phyllis related a story to her regarding an exceptional group of slaves who could fly and used this ability to resist the master's brutality and his religion. The story is based on a legend of Solomon

---

65. Drumgoold, "A Slave Girl's Story," 3.
66. Delaney, *From Darkness Cometh the Light*, 35.
67. Phyllis Green, quoted in Rawick, *The American Slave*, supplement 1, vol. 11, 180.

Legare Island. The legend says that a group of slaves were brought directly from Africa and given two weeks to "adjust themselves" to their new surroundings before being put to work. These slaves, according to the legend, noted Phyllis, were not ordinary beings. They refused to speak to others, they stayed to themselves, and "when dey left by dey self you could hear a tapping, tapping all day and all night." When the time came for the master to put them to work with the crack of the whip "[d]ey come out and dey stretch out dey han jees like dey gwine to tek de tools to wuk like de rest. But when dey stretch dey han dey rise. At middle day you could see dem far out ober de ocean. At sundown you could hear 'o voice, but dey couldn't shum no mo'. Dem gone home."[68] Phyllis's response to her mistress's question, regarding slaves having a better life style and religion in America, demonstrates the ambivalence of black women toward the religion and life in America. Black women during slavery and emancipation engaged in a counter-cultural appropriation of religion and oppressive traditions that empowered them to seek the possible for their lives.

Unlike the narratives of slavery, the theological themes are much more subtle in the selected emancipation narratives. While their passion for life is consistently grounded in their religion, these narratives contain more general references to God and religion than specific thematic presentations found in the selected slave narratives of the previous chapter.[69] Rather than specific theological themes, the counter-cultural appropriation of religion seen in the slave narratives is a sort of "Immanuel (*God with Us*) Theology" in the book-length emancipation narratives. I use this designation because in many of the narratives the women talk about God (rather than Jesus as in the slave narratives) being present with them in their struggles for emancipation and through the difficult times afterward. Jesus is most often referenced in relation to conversion experiences and not specifically as the one with them in times of trouble. For instance, Kate Drumgoold referred to God's presence with her on almost every page and paragraph of her narrative, but she spoke of Jesus primarily in relation to her conversion experience. Lucy Delaney most often referenced God as a Judge of the oppressor and the One able to correct the

---

68. Ibid., 179.

69. Although the ex-slave narratives are indexed topically and thematically, I did not choose my selected narratives based on the theological themes in them. My primary selection category was sexual and physical abuse. I wanted to discern from these texts the source of hope without imposing thematic thrust upon them. Will Coleman, Dwight Hopkins, George Cummings, and Delores Williams have thematically explored the ex-slave interviews. See Hopkins and Cummings, *Cut Loose Your Stammering Tongue*; Delores Williams, "Visions, Inner Voices, Apparitions, and Defiance in Nineteenth-Century Black Women's Narratives," *Women's Studies Quarterly* 21 (spring/summer 1993): 81–89.

injustices perpetrated against black women (and blacks in general). There is a distinct theo-centrism, rather than christo-centrism, in these narratives. However, we cannot overlook the tendency, even today, for black people to use God and Jesus interchangeably. References to God's presence can in fact mean Jesus or the Holy Spirit. This Trinitarian interchange is common in black religion.[70]

The ex-slave interviews do have some thematic elements that resemble the narratives written during slavery. Perhaps this similarity of content has to do with the focus on the same context. Although the ex-slave interviews were written in the 1930s, they focused on slavery. Thus, some of the same theological themes are consistent in the slave narratives and the ex-slave interviews. The pneumatological focus that was present in the slave narratives is also present in the ex-slave interviews, while there is very little reference to the Spirit in the book-length emancipation narratives. For example, Mary Gladdy attributed her ability to read and write to the Spirit coming upon her. Though she never attended school or was taught to read and write, she was able to read the Bible and write messages when the Spirit came upon her. Mary reported to her interviewer that she had frequent "visitations of the spirit" in the middle of the night. She was impelled to rise from her bed and write in an unknown hand. Her strange writing

> . . . covered over eighty pages of letter paper and bears a marked resemblance to crude shorthand notes. Offhand she can "cipher" about half of these strange writings; the other half, however, she can neither make heads nor tails, except when the spirit is upon her. When the spirit eases off, she again becomes ignorant of the significance of the mysterious half of her spirit-directed writings.[71]

Thus, her inability to read the Bible and to write and decipher the writing were transformed to supernatural ability when the Spirit overshadowed or visited her.

Another recurring theme in the ex-slave interviews was their ecclesiological focus. Most of the selected ex-slaves' interviews talk about the church and the slaves' persistent determination to worship (although they were often denied the right to worship the way they chose). Even when given the opportunity to go to church with whites, the women related that the women and men

---

70. Harold Carter discusses this tendency in *The Prayer Tradition of Black People* (Valley Forge, Penn.: Judson Press, 1976).

71. Mary Gladdy, quoted in Rawick, *The American Slave*, supplement, vol. 3, 257.

often held another worship service after sundown. Clara Brim, an ex-slave from Louisiana, indicated that there was a "bipartite religious system":

> When Sunday come Old Massa ask who want to go to church. Dem what wants could ride hoss-back or walk. Us go to de white folks church. Dey sot in front and us sot in back. Us had prayer meetin' too, regular every week. One old culled man a sort of preacher. He de leader in 'ligion.[72]

Phyllis Green related a tripartite religious system in her interview:

> You know when I been come home an' pass lat church on de corner, I hear de poor choir dis strainin so, an' aint a God's soul in dere to he'p em, an' when I look an' saw 'nough of people to come out, I say 'do Jesus is dat de best dey can do? Dat church been full up wid rustycats (aristocrats). Dem don't want to hear 'e boice (voice) but nebber mind when det (death) come den you hear dem sing. Dey dast not sing den. Den I gone on down de street an' pass an older church. I could hear dat preacher mos' two blocks. I aint mind hear em ef 'e stick to what he been wanna preach. 'E warn't any wish-pering (whispering) preacher, an' dem does sing in dat church as sweet an' loud as any colored people.
>
> In we church we pay em for hear 'e boice. I aint mind ef 'e mash me foot, I can draw em een (in) enty. I want em mash me foot ef I gib em 'casion.[73]

Not only was there a black church, and a white church but there was an aristocratic white church and another type of white church that more closely resembled black worship. Nonetheless, the interviews are full of references to worship that sustained the black community.

Perhaps it is significant that as the focus shifted away from slavery as the context of abuse and violence, the religious emphasis of hope weakened or at least changed. Those narratives that focus specifically on slavery (slave narratives and portions of the ex-slave interviews) contained stronger theological themes and a clearer counter-cultural appropriation of the dominant cultural religion as a ground for black women's hope. The portions of the ex-slave interviews that deal with emancipation and the book-length emancipation narratives still contain a hope that is grounded in religion, but the religious underpinning becomes more general in the selected narratives. Yet, the passion for the possible in black women's lives did not diminish. The Hope in the Holler was not extinguished. Involvement in church, society, social, and cultural movements to better the plight of her race and gender continued the

---

72. Clara Brim, quoted in Rawick, *The American Slave*, vol. 1, 34.
73. Phyllis Green, quoted in Rawick, *The American Slave*, supplement 1, vol. 11, 180–81.

momentum drawn from the late nineteenth and early twentieth century. By the mid-twentieth century, black women's narratives recorded the continued quest to overcome abuse and violence in the modern context. Stereotypical notions continue to inform the abuse of black women, and their religion continues to counter the oppressive nature of daily existence in a society that imposes slavery without chains. The narratives of contemporary women who have suffered sexual abuse and violence, to which we now turn, demonstrate the persistent passion for the possible in life that formulates a theology of hope in the narratives of black women.

Chapter 4

Hope in the Holler

*T*his chapter examines the narratives of contemporary African American women who have been victimized through physical or sexual violence. I explore African American women's hope in the midst of, or in spite of, abuse and violence from within, as well as outside, the African American community and church. During the contemporary period, the focus of black women's narratives shifted from the societal atrocities they suffered to the oppression heaped on them from within the black community and family. Perhaps as more laws, institutions, and civil rights organizations challenged the general oppression of black people and won legal battles to overcome discrimination and abuse, black women were unwilling to allow the exposure of only part of their oppression. They wrote to unmask and debunk all bastions of abuse, even if it meant exposing the injustice in the black family, church, or community. Taboos of revealing incest and abuse from within the community became the next frontier to be exposed. Statistics from the mid-nineteenth century forward show that, between the ages of nine and twelve, black females are more likely to be sexually abused than white females. Abuse usually occurs in the home of the victim by a trusted family member, friend, neighbor, or relative and at times has even been their minister.[1] In the lives of these women, hope often has a mediating function. It is a spiritual bridge, connecting the pains of their foremothers and their own personal struggles for renewed hope and liberated existence.

The trials and triumphs of slavery and emancipation are continued and enlarged upon during the contemporary period. I have dated the contemporary period from the post–World War II era forward, the 1950s through the present. Contemporary African American women continue the quest for

---

1. Evelyn C. White, ed., *The Black Women's Health Book: Speaking for Ourselves* (Seattle: Seal Press, 1990), 78.

humanity, autonomy, voice, and equality for which their foremothers struggled. The chapter argues that there are threads of connectedness between the struggles and hope of slavery and emancipation to the experiences of contemporary African American women, who have been abused. This will be established through an analysis of the narratives of several contemporary African American women, including Fannie Lou Hamer, Maya Angelou, Andrea Canaan, Linda Hollies, Melba Wilson, and Evelyn White. This analysis will focus on the influence of the changing context of abuse on the experiences of African American women and the content of their narratives. Next we will explore the contemporary mythologies that shape the image of African American women and serve to legitimize their continued abuse. The chapter then focuses on the struggles of contemporary African American women as recorded in their narratives, and concludes with the theological expressions and contemporary notions of hope voiced in these narratives.

Most of the contemporary women whose narratives we are exploring are still living today. Their voices speak for the thousands of black women who are enduring, surviving, and transforming situations of abuse and violence. These contemporary narratives make clear that the sex, class, and gender oppression of black women is unidirectional (in the church and in society) as well as bifocal (within the black community and from outside). We must now turn our attention to the contemporary context and its impact on the lives of black women.

The Changing Context of Abuse: The Contemporary Period

After the Great Depression and World War II, the United States embarked on a new era of freedom. The second world war had been fought for freedom from tyranny and oppression. President Franklin D. Roosevelt's four freedoms—freedom of speech, freedom of worship, freedom from want, and freedom from fear—became a part of the American ethos. Yet the reality was that black people were still being denied the very freedoms that had prompted this country to fight a war.

The civil rights movement of the 1950s and 1960s evokes such names as Dr. Martin Luther King Jr., Thurgood Marshall, Adam Clayton Powell, and Medgar Evers—all men. However, as historian Charles Payne notes, prior to 1964 there were considerably more *women* involved in the civil rights movement than men. Indeed, women outnumbered men three or four to one. Women were the organizers of the movement, not just fund-raisers and supporters of the cause. There was good reason why women were disproportionately involved in the early civil rights struggles:

The answer to the question of why black women were disproportionately involved in the day-to-day activities of the early civil rights struggle appears to lie, first in the participation of black women in religious and community activities and, second, in their cultural preparation for resistance. Black women in the 1930s and 1960s knew how to organize, were accustomed to working together, and felt a strong kinship with members of the community beyond their immediate families. The church and the community work in which they had been involved for two centuries—and especially in the sixty years before the Civil Rights movement—made them ideal political activists.[2]

Though their names were seldom called and their faces rarely recognized by the masses, black women were at the forefront of the civil rights movement. Ella Baker, Fannie Lou Hamer, Nannie Helen Burroughs, and Rosa Parks were but a few of the "head-ragged generals" that led the fight for equality and rights during this period.

While many events during the 1950s and 1960s foreshadowed the changing tide of America, the death of Emmett Till, litigation by the NAACP on behalf of black rights, and the bus boycott of Montgomery, Alabama, are three significant events. Emmett Till was a black teenager who lived in Chicago with his mother, Mamie Bradley. Emmett went to visit relatives in Mississippi. He was violently killed because when asked what he thought of a white lady in a general store, he whistled his approval. The woman's husband and son considered this a sign of disrespect to a white woman. They took him to the woods, shot him in the head, tied a seventy-pound cotton gin around his neck, and dumped him in the river. The two men were tried and found not guilty.[3]

Upon seeing her son's body, Mamie Bradley collapsed, but she resolved that this crime would not be hidden. She was determined to "place her suffering in the collective consciousness of the black community."[4] Rather than grieving silently with a few friends and family, hoping for the horror to just dissipate, Mamie delayed the burial of her son and allowed *Jet*, a prominent nationally circulated black magazine, to photograph and publish pictures of her son's mutilated, waterlogged body. She also delayed the burial of her son by four days so that thousands of people could view his body, and she added "to let the world see what they did to my boy."[5] This incident had an enormous

---

2. Darlene Clark Hine and Kathleen Thompson, eds., *The Shining Thread of Hope: The History of Black Women in America* (New York: Broadway Books, 1998), 267–68.

3. See the story of Emmett Till in *Eyes on the Prize: The American Civil Rights Years, 1954–1965*, ed. Juan Williams (New York: Viking Penguin, 1987), 43–47.

4. Hine and Thompson, *The Shining Thread of Hope*, 270.

5. Ibid., 270.

effect on black women across the nation and increased their resolve to fight for equality, education, and human freedom. Myrlie Evers Williams recalled:

> I bled for Emmett Till's mother. I know when she came to Mississippi and appeared at mass meetings how everyone poured out their hearts to her, went into their pockets when people only had two or three pennies, and gave . . . some way to say that we bleed for you, we are so sorry about what happened to Emmett. And this is just one thing that will be a frame of reference for us to move on to do more things, positively, to eliminate this from happening ever again.[6]

The fight for equality, education, and freedom rested on their faith in a God who loved all people. Mamie stated that she did not hate the people who had done this to her son and could raise their children and love them, yet her attitude was not one of mere acceptance. She resolved, and encouraged other black women, to get an education because that, for her, was the key to freedom. Her attitude "was one shared by millions of black women whose spiritual heritage gave them the strength to fight back in the decade to come."[7] There was Hope in the Holler.

The early 1950s and 1960s were also a time of legal battles for the rights of blacks that gained national attention. Many of these battles were initiated by the NAACP. A major front was the quest for equal education for blacks. In 1952 Barbara Johns challenged the "equal" part of the "separate but equal" policy of her high school in Prince Edward, Virginia. Barbara's life was threatened and she was forced to move to Montgomery with her uncle, Vernon Johns. Johns was the pastor of Dexter Avenue Baptist Church. Upon his retirement in 1954 he was succeeded by the new pastor, Dr. Martin Luther King Jr. The Johns case preempted several other legal battles, including the case that challenged the "separate but equal" precedent set by the *Plessy v. Ferguson* case. The most famous of the cases was *Brown v. the Board of Education*. Separate but equal was ruled as unjust in that public education for blacks was rarely equal to that provided for whites. But the battle for equal rights extended beyond the educational arena and involved courtrooms, lawyers, or universities. The next phase of the battle, and the pivotal point of the civil rights movement, was led and organized by black women.

Rosa Parks was one of several black women who were trailblazers in the fights for equality and rights for black women and black humanity in general.[8]

---

6. Ibid.
7. Ibid., 271.
8. An excellent series of articles on black women in the civil rights movement can be found in *Women in the Civil Rights Movement: Trailblazers & Torchbearers, 1941–1965*, ed. Vicki L. Crawford, Jacqueline Anne Rouse, and Barbara Woods (Bloomington: Indiana University Press, 1993).

Many of them had experienced the humiliation of paying money to ride the city bus and yet being denied a seat if a white person needed one. Though one of many, Rosa Parks was the woman around which the Montgomery bus boycott centered. Rosa Parks refused to give up her seat to a white man after a long day's work. She was dragged off the bus, and arrested for her "crime." She remarked that she had experienced "a life history of being rebellious against being mistreated because of my color. . . . I had pushed as far as I could stand to be pushed. . . . I had decided that I would have to know once and for all what rights I had as a human being and as a citizen."[9] Her arrest ignited the civil rights movement and the public leadership of Dr. Martin Luther King Jr. However, it was a woman, Jo Ann Robinson, who had written letters to civil rights leaders about this issue. She developed and passed out flyers about Parks's arrest and the need for blacks to demand their rights. She also made the suggestion that blacks boycott the buses to demonstrate their economic power.[10] The male leadership came to the fore of the movement, and the women who organized, implemented, and supported the boycott were obscured. The sexism confronting black women in the black community was usually subservient to the battles against racism in the larger societal context. Yet, the external battles against injustices in society brought into clearer focus the need to openly confront the injustices inside the community.

The tension between black women and black men, between their role in the church as well as in the public arena, was not new. But the recording of this victimization from within the black community emerges more readily in contemporary black women's narratives. The struggles of black women in the church had been recorded for decades in the narratives of women like Jarena Lee and Old Elizabeth, who preached the gospel to wide audiences in spite of opposition from male leadership in the black church. But the sexual exploitation of black women from within the black community had remained hidden from their pages. The sexual revolution of the 1960s made it more acceptable to even talk about sex. As we move to the narratives of the 1970s and forward, the topic of abuse and violence became more central. The context of abuse not only included the white community, but victimization came from within the black community as well. I am not suggesting that abuse of black women by black men did not occur prior to the '70s. What I am saying is that, in the selected narratives, abuse and violence from within the black community was

---

9. As quoted in *Black Women in America: An Historical Encyclopedia*, vol. 2, ed. Darlene Clark Hine, Elsa Barkley Brown, Rosalyn Terborg-Penn (Bloomington: Indiana University Press, 1994), 808.

10. For an excellent source of Robinson's crucial involvement in the organization of the Montgomery bus boycott, see David J. Garrow, ed., *The Montgomery Bus Boycott and the Women Who Started It: The Memoir of Jo Ann Gibson Robinson* (Knoxville: University of Tennessee Press, 1987).

not talked about or recorded prior to the contemporary period. Nor am I suggesting that the abuse of contemporary black women comes only from within the black community. Race, class, and gender oppression by white males and females is an ongoing part of the dilemma for blacks in America. Yet, one can turn to the narratives of abused black women to understand their ability to embody hope in this changing context of abuse.

Before we explore the selected contemporary narratives, it is necessary to consider the myths regarding black women that existed during this period. As during slavery and emancipation, the myths about black women influenced their treatment and the subsequent content of their narratives.

Contemporary Sexualized Myths
Regarding African American Women

The contemporary period has its own sexualized myths about black women. The contemporary characterizations evolved from the myths of slavery and emancipation. The Jezebel and Mammy myths of slavery continued during emancipation and reemerged as the Negro wench and Aunt Jemima portrayals of black women. Eventually the "bad black woman" myth—a hypersexual black woman whose morals excluded her from protection by the law—became a popular depiction of black women also. But the most pervasive stereotype of black women during the twentieth century is the Sapphire mythology. The Sapphire mythology depicts black women as bossy, loud, dominating women who emasculate black men. Hers is an asexual, but nonetheless consuming, posture. Whereas Jezebel emasculated men by stripping them of their ability to resist her seductive sexual persona, Sapphire, on the other hand, emasculates black men by aggressively usurping their roles. She is strong, controlling, and efficient like Mammy, but lacks the compassion and willingness to function within prescribed boundaries for black women, as Mammy did. Sapphire also lacks the maternal compassion of Mammy, making her a competitive challenger to the "man's world."

Like the mythologies that we have explored in the previous chapters, the Sapphire myth developed over a period of time and became more widely circulated and embraced through modern technology and "scientific" data. The genesis of Sapphire dates back to a radio program that became popular in the late 1920s, the *Amos 'n' Andy Show*. The show depicted two southern black men who had moved north to Chicago. It was aired by NBS Radio and became its most popular show by 1929. The show became a national obsession. Two of the characters, Kingfish and his wife, Sapphire, were the pivotal figures of the episodes. In 1951 the television version of the show made its debut on CBS. The show was immediately denounced by the NAACP as a demeaning and derogatory stereotypical depiction of black people. A tremendous controversy arose surrounding the show, yet it won an Emmy nomination in 1952. CBS canceled the show after its second season, but the syndicated versions of it aired until the mid-1960s and became a staple of American television.[11]

During the airing of the *Amos 'n' Andy Show*, Sapphire became its most popular, most stereotypical female character. She was the domineering, sharp-tongued, emasculating wife of Kingfish. She embodied most of the stereo-types about black women that were prevalent, an extension of the "bad black woman" characterization. Sapphire often scolded her husband for being unreliable, lazy, and dishonest. Thus, her characterization also reinforced the myths about black men. Sapphire and Kingfish etched into the psyches of millions of white and black Americans the notion of discord between passive, shiftless black men and aggressive, dominating black women. *Sapphire* became a pervasive term for emasculating black women, and is a stereotype that persists in the contemporary conception of black women.

The Sapphire stereotype was embraced in the African American, as well as in the white, community. It has been "validated" through inaccurate historical interpretations of black women's experiences. Black sociologist E. Franklin Frazier's work was foundational to this misconception. In 1939, Frazier published *The Negro Family in the United States*. He remarked in his book that "the Negro woman as wife or mother was the mistress of her cabin, and save for interference of master or overseer, her wishes in regard to mating and family matters were paramount."[12] Frazier cast the black family as a matriarchal institution. Daniel Moynihan published a study of the black family in 1954 that was partially based on the work of Frazier. Moynihan concluded that traditional roles of husband and wife (in white families) were often reversed in the American Negro family. He asserted that black families were matriarchal. Moynihan asserted that the role reversal in the Negro family was so debilitating and emasculating for black men that they should run to the armed forces for refuge, away from black women.[13]

Frazier and Moynihan believed that black women controlled black families by dominating black men and controlling the sexual relations. Frazier

---

11. Hine, Brown, Terborg-Penn, eds., *Black Women in America*, 1009.

12. E. Franklin Frazier, *The Negro Family in the United States* (Chicago: University of Chicago Press, 1939), 125; as quoted in Deborah Gray White, *Ar'n't I a Woman? Female Slaves in the Plantation South* (New York: W. W. Norton, 1985), 166.

13. Daniel Patrick Moynihan, *The Negro Family, the Case for National Action* (Washington, D.C.: Office of Policy Planning and Research, 1965), 30–31, 42.

even used the term *mating*, typically used to refer to the sexual practices of animals, for the sexual activity between a black man and woman. He suggested that there was a hierarchy of control in the family, the overseer or master, black women, then black men. Moynihan echoed Frazier's findings by suggesting that separatism was the only hope of saving black males from the dominating grip of the black women. Through media such as the radio and television versions of *Amos 'n' Andy*, and "scientific books" such as those by Franklin and Moynihan, the stereotypical image of Sapphire, the dominating emasculating black woman, became etched in the American psyche.

Another twentieth-century stereotype that persists is the "superwoman" myth. Linda Hollies uses this stereotype in her narrative to describe her mother, whom she calls "the total woman." Her mother was able to cook, clean, take care of home and husband. She was always neat, never wore her hair in rollers, and was there for everyone, wherever and whenever they needed her.[14]

Unlike the other myths that we have explored, this stereotype is readily embraced by many contemporary black women. This myth, more than any of the others we have examined, facilitates the silence around abuse and violence in the black community. Black women have been expected to bear all and tell nothing, even when the perpetrator lives under the same roof. Black women were without legal recourse during slavery and emancipation, so they often were forced to bear abuse in silence. But the demand for silence around abuse and violence also has roots in the black community, which has, for decades, been forced to fight for voice regarding its oppression by the dominant society. The unity of the black community has centered around standing together, supporting one another, and a kind of understood loyalty that does not allow one to air "dirty laundry."

The tendency toward bearing the burden of abuse, whether self-imposed or forced, is a psychological and theological residual of slavery. Silence, black identity issues, and rage have been identified as the hallmarks of oppression and a psychological residual of slavery. Slaves were made to watch the oppression of other slaves and forced to remain silent about the abuse in total deference to the master. Psychologically, this reinforced a sense of powerlessness and a lack of voice in the slave. Ken Hardy argues that all experiences of the African American are shaded by the residuals of slavery. Silence, the hallmark of oppression, is expressed today in the fact that many African

---

14. See Michele Wallace's discussion of the topic in her book, *Black Macho and the Myth of the Superwoman* (London: John Cader Press, 1979), 107.

Americans do not feel empowered to articulate their views and still opt to suffer in silence.[15]

Not only are psychological residuals of slavery evident today, but there are theological residuals as well. The theological residuals of slavery include the counter-cultural appropriation of Scripture, the centrality of experience as a vehicle for interpreting divine revelation, and the misuse of power and Scripture to justify physical, spiritual, and emotional abuse. The Bible is now, and always has been, a critical source for theological understanding for black people. When the slave masters misused the Pauline injunction, "slaves be obedient to your masters" (Eph. 6:5–8 KJV), slaves did not reject the Bible. They looked to the example of Jesus, and through his life were able to reappropriate the text in light of their experience.[16] Just as the slave masters attempted to ensure behavior through scriptural injunctions, we will find as we look at the experiences of contemporary women that Scripture was often used to justify their abuse. This justification, however, does not come only from the white male dominant society, but also from within the black community, and serves to reinforce the bear-all, tell-nothing myth of the superwoman.

The Victimization of Contemporary African American Women

I assert that we must go to the voices of contemporary black women to glean their experiences of abuse and that which enabled them to overcome victimization. Further, I assert that as the context of abuse changed so did the content of their narratives and the function of "hope" in their lives. We now turn to the voices of contemporary women to hear their experiences of abuse and how they endured, survived, and at times transformed their lives and their communities into vessels of hope.

Fannie Lou Hamer is a sort of contemporary Sojourner Truth. Like Sojourner, her life spans two critical periods in the history of black women: the post-emancipation and the civil rights eras. She was born Fannie Lou Townsend in 1917 in the Mississippi Delta area. She was a young child during the Great Depression and a young woman during World War II. Fannie Lou lived in the South and experienced the new slavery, sharecropping. From

---

15. Kenneth Hardy, *The Psychological Residuals of Slavery*, video produced by Stephen Lerner, (Topeka, Kan.: Equal Partners Productions, 1995).

16. See the discussion of the *Haustafeln* and slavery in Cain Hope Felder, *Stoney the Road We Trod: African American Biblical Interpretation* (Minneapolis: Fortress Press, 1991), 213–18.

age six she worked in the cotton fields of a Mississippi plantation, chopping and picking cotton. When the plantation owner discovered she could read and write (in 1944), he made her timekeeper and record-keeper for the plantation. Fannie Lou married Perry Hamer in 1945. Mrs. Hamer continued to work as a timekeeper and recordkeeper on the Marlow plantation until the early 1960s. Her life changed with the advent of the fight for voting rights for black people in Mississippi. She was forty-four years old and yet she could not vote.

The Mississippi Delta was a particularly difficult place for blacks. They did not have access to the "American Dream" of the 1960s. Though blacks lacked the right to vote, few were concerned about voting because they were busy struggling for the basic necessities of life. Most blacks did not have jobs and lacked proper schooling to obtain a decent job. They were hungry, lived in inadequate housing, and had no access to health care. They were the target of brutality; dogs were let out on them; it was not safe to travel after dark; and sometimes homes were burned down at night. Few blacks were eager to become publicly involved in the civil rights work of the NAACP, or any other group, because of the economic and physical reprisals that were perpetrated against blacks.

The victimization of Fannie Lou Hamer preceded her public life and the abuse she experienced as a result of her activism on voters rights. When Hamer was forty-two years old, she went to the doctor, complaining of abdominal pain. She was diagnosed as having a uterine tumor and was admitted to the hospital to have the tumor removed. She later discovered that she had been sterilized. The doctor performed a hysterectomy without her knowledge or consent. Hamer began spreading the word about black women being sterilized without their knowledge or consent. Her anger at the lack of control over her body and her life fueled her determination to gain her rights. When asked why she did not sue the doctor, she replied, "At that time? Me? Getting a white lawyer to go against a white doctor?" She told Young, "I would have been taking my hands and screwing tacks in my own casket."[17]

The sterilization of poor black women came to national attention as black women began to file lawsuits to stop such treatment. One such case was the sterilization of two poor black girls at an Alabama family-planning clinic. The girls, who were sisters, were only twelve and fourteen. Their mother, who could not read or write, signed what she thought was consent for anti-fertility shots. Instead of receiving anti-fertility shots, they were taken into a room and sterilized.[18] Their lawsuit brought national attention to the involuntary steril-

17. Perry Deane Young, "A Surfeit of Surgery," *Washington Post*, 30 May 1976, B1, as cited in Kay Mills, *This Little Light of Mine: The Life of Fannie Lou Hamer* (New York: Penguin Books, 1993), 22.
18. Ibid., 21–22.

ization of poor black women—a situation of which poor rural black women, like Fannie Lou Hamer, had long been aware.

Not only did Hamer experience involuntary sterilization, she was also severely beaten for her activities in the voter's rights campaigns. When the young civil rights workers of the Student Nonviolent Coordinating Committee (SNCC) arrived in Ruleville, Mississippi, looking for people who were willing to try to register to vote, Hamer volunteered without hesitation. When she returned from her unsuccessful attempt to register to vote, Mr. Marlow, for whom she had worked for eighteen years, put her and her husband off his plantation. They lived with friends, frequently moving from house to house in fear of the violence their presence attracted. On one of the trips to the courthouse to take black people to register to vote, the whole group was detained and jailed by Winona police. Hamer was separated from the other women, and she and some of the other women were beaten. The guards of the jail took two black male inmates and told them to beat Hamer or they would beat them They watched to be sure their instructions were carried out to their satisfaction. When the inmate told Hamer to lie on the bed, she asked him, "You mean you would do this to your own race?" "So then I had to get over on the bed flat on my stomach, and that man beat me—that man beat me until he give out."[19] Hamer's body was severely bruised from head to toe, she was swollen and in tremendous pain, yet she and the others who were beaten were denied medical treatment. As a result of this beating, Hamer suffered physically the rest of her life from kidney problems and blood clots that diminished the sight in her right eye.[20] Still, Hamer continued her quest for rights and became an active part of the voters registration movement in Mississippi and a national spokesperson on behalf of poor black Americans, women and men.

Maya Angelou was born Marguerite Johnson to Bailey and Vivian (Baxter) Johnson in St. Louis, Missouri, in 1928. Her narrative brings to light the struggle for autonomy and equality in her own community as well as the larger society. Angelou's narrative graphically captures sexual abuse from within the black community. As the statistics cited at the beginning of the chapter indicated, she was raped by a person known to her, whom she had learned to trust and respect, a "friend" of the family. Her experience was a preview of the experiences of many contemporary black women. Angelou's narrative was one of the earliest recordings of incest in the black community. Many disapproved of Angelou exposing the black community; she notes, "A number of people have asked me why I wrote about the rape in *I Know Why the Caged*

---

19. Mills, *This Little Light of Mine*, 60.
20. Ibid., 93.

Bird Sings. They wanted to know why I had to tell that rape happens in the black community."[21] Incest survivor Melba Wilson noted that Angelou's courage to tell her story broke the silence in the black community about incest:

> Reading the first installment of Maya Angelou's autobiography, more than twenty years ago now, was my first encounter with incest in the black community in print. . . . I would like to publicly thank [her] for having the courage to break the taboo of silence, an outgrowth of which was to reach women like me, who needed their stories in order to find the strength to tell our own.[22]

Perhaps Angelou's narrative was the catalyst for the writing of accounts of incestuous abuse by a number of twentieth-century black women. The proliferation of narratives and fiction in the twentieth century that document incest could attest to this fact.[23]

Angelou's parents divorced when she was three years old and her brother, Bailey, was four. The two children were sent to live with their paternal grandmother in Stamps, Arkansas. Though they were living through the depression in the South, her grandmother was able to provide for their needs through a small general store she owned.[24] It was her grandmother who taught her "common sense, practicality and the ability to control one's own destiny that comes through constant hard work and courage."[25] Her grandmother provided her with love, a strong sense of black tradition, and a reliance on the black church. But the childhood innocence, security, and love that she had gleaned from her grandmother was shattered on a visit to her mother, who at the time lived in St. Louis. Maya was only seven years old when she went to visit her mother. The eight-month stay disrupted her life. Maya, at the age of eight, was raped by her mother's boyfriend.[26] He silenced Maya by threatening her, "[I]f you scream I'm going to kill you. And if you tell I'm going to kill Bailey."[27] The rape was discovered, and Mr. Freeman, the mother's boyfriend, was arrested. He was sentenced to one year and one day for this heinous crime. He never served one day because his lawyer got him released the same afternoon. Maya recalled playing Monopoly in the living room with her brother Bailey when a

21. Maya Angelou in *Black Women Writers at Work*, ed. Claudia Tate (New York: Continuum, 1983).

22. Melba Wilson, *Crossing the Boundary: Black Women Survive Incest* (Seattle: Seal Press, 1993), 40.

23. A few black female authors who have written about incest in their work are Buchi Emecheta, Alice Walker, and Joan Riley, as well as the women whose narratives are cited in this chapter.

24. Maya Angelou, *I Know Why the Caged Bird Sings* (New York: Random House, 1970), 3–7.

25. As quoted in Jessie Carney Smith, *Epic Lives: One Hundred Black Women Who Made a Difference* (Detroit: Visible Ink Press, 1993), 11.

26. Angelou, *I Know Why the Caged Bird Sings*, 64–74.

27. Ibid., 64.

policeman knocked at the door. She noted "the man in the living room was taller than the sky and whiter than my image of God. He just didn't have a beard."[28] He had come to tell Mrs. Baxter that Freeman had been found dead, kicked to death and left in a vacant lot. Maya overheard the conversation and came to the conclusion that it was her words that had caused his death:

> In those moments I decided that although Bailey loved me he couldn't help me. I had sold myself to the devil and there could be no escape. The only thing I could do was to stop talking to people other than Bailey. Instinctively, or somehow, I knew that because I loved him so much I couldn't hurt him, but if I talked to anyone else that person might die too. Just my breath, carrying my words out, might poison people and they'd curl up and die.[29]

Maya became a self-imposed mute for five years. She believed that her words meant death to anyone who heard them, except Bailey. Just as she had decided to be silent, she decided when to speak again. Even at eight years old, she was determined to maintain control over something in her life, even if she had lost control of her body. Maya emerged from her silent cocoon to become a literary genius, whose faith-inspired words are life-giving to African American women, and children, and humanity in general.

For Andrea Canaan, abuse moved beyond the circle of friend and neighbors. Her abuse involved the sacred. Andrea was raped by a Methodist minister just before her twelfth birthday. She recorded the devastating effects of the abuse on her psyche and soul. "I did not dream the loss," she says. "I did not make up the guilt, force my separation from God, my church, my community. I did not imagine the shame, the judgement, the cold silence and distance. That I was placed apart and blamed is real."[30] Andrea's narrative moves to the topic of clergy misconduct and the abuse of power in the church. Her narrative also reveals another seldom-discussed topic in the black community: sexual abuse by black women. Andrea mentions in her narrative that she was abused by two women, her mother and a church camp counselor. She does not give the details of this abuse, but alludes to her mother's abuse as *knowing* of her abuse but not *stopping* it. Andrea is prompted to tell her story, she says, to release the secrets and transgress the "no tell" rules. "I am honoring my courage and strength during those nightmare years. I am grateful to myself for saving my life until this time when I can remember, name and become

28. Ibid., 71.
29. Ibid., 73.
30. Andrea Canaan, "I Call Up Names: Facing Childhood Sexual Abuse," in *The Black Women's Health Book*, 79.

myself. . . . I pray these truths will afford my daughter no betrayal at my own hand, nor any betrayal that I know of and will not stop."[31] Like many of the contemporary women's narratives, her passion is centered on recapturing the self, created in the image of God that is worthy of healthy love, as well as freedom from the guilt, shame, and silence of abuse.

Linda Hollies was also abused by a minister, but this minister was her father. Hollies used a biblical metaphor to describe her abuse; she called it a mountain. "There has been a gigantic mountain in my life since the age of twelve or thirteen. This mountain could not be moved, and it was too overwhelming for me, a child, to attempt to climb."[32] This is an allusion to biblical text that says, "You will say to this mountain, 'Move from here to there,' and it will move" (Matt. 17:20) and the Negro spiritual that says, "Lord, don't move this mountain, just give me the strength to climb." The mountain of abuse from her father seemed to her for many years unmovable. Hollies's description of his behavior is reminiscent of the slave masters described in chapter 2:

> He was a very angry man. He was called, "Thor, the god of thunder" by his children. He yelled, screamed and hurled insult upon insult at us. His demeanor was seldom pleasant, either at home or away; he was a strict disciplinarian and quick to whip with the handy strap. He was emotionally, physically, and mentally abusive to me and my seven siblings; his behavior toward my mother was the same. I cannot remember one kind or encouraging remark my father ever made to me; my accomplishments were usually belittled or ignored.[33]

The atmosphere in her home was so oppressive that Hollies likened her home to a slave camp. "The atmosphere in our home was perhaps similar to a slave labor camp, with my father as master and my mother as overseer. There were no loving relationships; we related to our father out of fear and to my mother out of respect. My father used the word love to justify his cruel behavior."[34] When asked by her father if she loved him, she answered honestly and said no. He slapped her and said, "Little saved girl, you *must* love your father and respect him as well."

Hollies also raises the issue of the theological impact of abuse and the appropriation of Scripture. "The act of incest alone is enough to cause one psycho-

---

31. Ibid., 81.
32. Linda Hollies, "A Daughter Survives Incest: A Retrospective Analysis," in *The Black Women's Health Book*, 82.
33. Hollies, "A Daughter Survives," 82.
34. Ibid., 84.

logical trauma and lifelong emotional damage, but when coupled with heavy theological ramifications, one is in double-trouble," she writes. Her father's favorite texts were about God's love. Children's disobedience and respect for parents were another favorite topic. He frequently discussed the topic, she notes, of the sinner's abode in hell. Another favorite of his was "the story of Lot and his two daughters, who had sex with him after they made him drunk, to perpetuate his lineage." This justification of abuse with Scripture created a theological dilemma, even for a twelve-year-old. "Well I had problems. I could not love this man who came into my bedroom and did unmentionable things to me; I could not believe that God could love me and yet allow this to continue. I surely had no respect for my father as a parent. Therefore, I was a sinner, right?"[35] Again the use of Scripture to justify abuse recalls the slave master's misapplication of the Pauline text, "Slaves be obedient to your masters," that was often used to justify slavery. Hollies's comment above elucidates the theological homelessness that is often generated in black women who have been abused. Theological homelessness is reinforced when Scripture is used to justify the abuse and silence the voice of the abused. The Bible is a critical source of hope and courage for black women. When the instrument of hope is disfigured into the tool of oppression, it is difficult to find other theological resources. Thus, many contemporary black women who have been abused, particularly by persons within the black community or church, find remaining in the church or denomination a difficult and sometimes impossible position for their healing. Their damaged self-image is a reflection of the damaged God image. The damaged image of self in relation to God leads to a theological holler, a cry for meaning, help, and hope to remove the "mountain" in their lives.

It is through a reappropriation of Scripture and the meaning of God's love that Hollies eventually begins to chip away at her mountain. Her passion is centered, first, on gaining personal wholeness, and then using her story as a means of breaking the silence of incest in the black community with the intent of liberating other women.

> I have grown to understand and to accept that the mountain will always be a part of my history—there is no magic "memory eraser." I have come to accept the strength of being a survivor. . . . I have accepted as a gift the grace of God that allows me to come through this situation with determination not only to help myself, but to reach out to others with mountains in their lives they cannot name. . . . Sharing my story gives hope to others and it also reaffirms the value of who I am.[36]

---

35. Ibid., 83.
36. Ibid., 90.

In spite of the abuse of her body and the disruption of her faith, Hollies affirms her empowering hope to survive and transform her situation. The passion for the possible in this life is the Hope in spite of the Holler that resulted from the abuse.

Melba Wilson was born in Virginia and reared in Texas. A survivor of incest, she was raped when she was a teenager by a black male who was a prominent official in the community. After the rape she sought medical assistance and direction from a doctor in the community. Because of the attacker's status in the community, she was not sure that she would be believed. The doctor's response to her cry for help was to put her on tranquilizers.[37] Wilson interweaves her personal narrative in her book, which focuses on the abuse of black women. Wilson wrote to expose the well-hidden secret of rape and incest in the black community. She acknowledges several women for whom she writes. Among them are

> . . . all those other young black girls out there who grew up into womanhood with their own heavy secrets, thinking they, too, were the only ones. I write, also, for their grown up counterparts who still carry that misused and abused little girl within them, because there was nowhere else for her go to.[38]

She writes for those who are emotional prisoners of the Holler. For Wilson, black women call upon "centuries-old strengths" that enable them to triumph over "centuries-old adversities."[39]

Hope in the Holler

Though abuse and violence have permeated the lives of many African American women, there is still Hope in their Holler. The Holler is the cry to right wrongs, to rectify injustices, and to gain respect for their disrespected bodies. The Holler is the refusal to be silenced, ignored, or dismissed. The Hope is our unquenchable passion and undauntable power that connects black women across the centuries. This bridge moves African American women from survival to the renewal of self and community. This transgenerational character of hope is reflected in contemporary women narratives. Maya Angelou reflects on her struggle for hope-filled existence. "The Black [sic] female is

---

37. Wilson, *Crossing the Boundary*, 31.
38. Ibid., 4.
39. Wilson, *Crossing the Boundary*, 38.

assaulted by all the forces of nature at the same time that she is caught in the tripartite crossfire of masculine prejudice, white [*sic*] illogical hate and Black [*sic*] lack of power."[40] The fact that African American women have had to have an enormous hope which affirms their humanity, power, and potential is observed by Angelou. She declares, "[T]he fact that the adult American Negro female emerges a formidable character is often met with amazement, distaste and even bewilderment. It is seldom accepted as an inevitable outcome of the struggle won by survivors and deserves respect if not enthusiastic acceptance."[41] Though life in the United States has been difficult for African American women, Angelou asserts that hope has been maldistributed, present in inordinate amounts, to counter inordinate oppression. The struggles of life in America have been "borne with dignity, and changed by hope. . . . [t]hey (African American women) have wept over their hopeless fate and defied destiny by creating hope anew."[42]

Religious beliefs have played a key role in African American women's ability to create hope anew. Fannie Lou Hamer was known for her bold, courageous speeches and her fervent, heartfelt singing. One of her favorite songs, which eventually became her theme, was "This Little Light of Mine, I'm Going to Let It Shine." Hamer told a civil rights worker:

> Singing is one of the main things that can keep us going. When you're in a brick cell, locked up, and haven't done anything to anybody but still you're locked up there and sometimes words just begin to come to you and you begin to sing. Like one of my favorite songs, "This Little Light of Mine, I'm Going to Let It Shine." This same song goes back to the fifth chapter of Matthew, which is the Beatitudes of the Bible, when he says a city that sits on a hill cannot be hid. Let your light so shine that men will see your good works and glorify the father which is in heaven. I think singing is very important. It brings out the soul.[43]

Hamer's passion for the possible in this life, her hope, was undergirded by her faith in Jesus Christ, who was, for her, the example of how black people were called to live. For Hamer, Christ "was a revolutionary person, out there where it was happening. That's what God is all about, and that's where I get my strength."[44] Her strength and her faith gave no place for hatred or violence,

---

40. Angelou, *I Know Why the Caged Bird Sings*, 231.

41. Ibid.

42. Emily Herring Wilson, *Hope and Dignity: Older Black Women of the South*, with an introduction by Maya Angelou (Philadelphia: Temple University Press, 1983), xii–xiii.

43. Taped interview with Dale Gronemeier, summer, 1964; as cited in Mills, *This Little Light of Mine*, 21.

44. Mills, *This Little Light of Mine*, 18.

though she had experienced both. After she was brutally beaten in the Winona jail, she said that she could not hate the abusers. Andrew Young, a civil rights worker who was with Hamer, commented after the beating: "She was instinctively an extremely nonviolent person who really was so polite and was so generous to her jailers, for instance—the people who had been beating her."[45] Hamer asserted, "It won't solve any problem for me to hate white people because they hate me. Oh there is so much hate! Only God has kept the Negro sane. . . . Regardless of what they act like, there's some good there. How can we say we love God and hate our brothers and sisters?"[46] Though she was threatened, shot at, beaten, and insulted, Hamer did not encourage grassroot people to use violence to gain their rights. For her, determination, faith, and songs were the keys to black people living God's kingdom on earth.

Though Hamer's faith was her bulwark, she had little regard for clergy or the church. She felt that the clergy were timid and had not taken a proper lead to gain the right to register to vote for black people. Regarding church, she added, "the most disturbing hour in the country is 11:00 A.M. Sunday morning when hypocrites from all walks of life converge on our churches for the sake of paying the minister's way to hell and theirs too. . . . She told her Harvard audience, churches must translate their ideals into practical action. If Jesus was here now, he'd be called a militant because he was where it was at, right down with the grass roots."[47] Yet Hamer worked closely with the church, usually holding meetings at the church because it was the only place black people could meet and whites would not become suspicious. Empowered by her faith, Hamer said she was "sick and tired of being sick and tired"[48] and fought relentlessly for the equal rights of blacks because black people's strength, tenacity, and faith made them the "hope of America." Hamer talked about the spirit of sacrifice in young people. She understood this as consistent with the christocentric model:

A living example was Andy Goodman, James Chaney and Michael Schwerner that come down here. And I remember talking to them the Sunday before they went to Oxford, Ohio, for the orientation where we had to drill or talk to them about what they might be faced with. Even when Christ hung on the cross, he said no greater love has no man than the one who is willing to lay down his life for his friends. Even though they were aware they might

45. Ibid., 17.
46. Ibid., 98.
47. Ibid., 238.
48. This became the most frequently quoted saying of Hamer and is documented in many publications, interviews, and books about her life. See Mills, *This Little Light of Mine*, 93.

die, they still came. These are the things we have to think about. These are the things we can't sweep under the rug. And these are the things that still gave me hope.[49]

Hamer's hope was rooted in living the life of Jesus, of revolutionary involvement coupled with love.

Andrea Canaan and Linda Hollies were both abused by ministers, representatives of the gospel. Yet their counter-appropriation of the gospel enabled them to survive and work to transform the lives of other black women by breaking the silence surrounding abuse in the black church and the black community. The counter-appropriation of the gospel is not in response to the white religious teachings; rather, it is counter to the misappropriation of the text by their black male abusers. Andrea's initial response to her minister's "gospel" was to feel separated from God, her church, and her community. But, in a letter to her mother, which Andrea wrote as an adult, Andrea acknowledges her reconnectedness to God and the community. She claims her strength and courage to overcome the trauma in her life. In a poem at the end of her letter, she names those who have helped her find the way:

In the name of the Goddesses and Gods known and unknown, named and unnamed,
    In the name of my foremothers and forefathers known and unknown, named and unnamed,
    In the name of my brothers and sisters, my friends and my lovers, my daughters and sons, those who died so young and those who are yet living.
    I pray that I continue to break the cycles of madness visited man upon woman, man upon man, woman upon woman, woman upon man, father upon daughter and son, mother upon son and daughter, kin and neighbor against each other. I pray these truths. . . . I am woman who is child no longer, woman who is making herself sane, whole.[50]

Canaan combines the spiritual and cultural. She calls upon the Goddesses and Gods as well as the ancestors and the community. Her passion centers around personal wholeness, transforming a fragmented shame and guilt-ridden victim into a courageous, life-affirming vessel.

Linda Hollies rejected the God of her abusive father, who was a pentecostal minister. She found a God of love in the United Methodist Church. Linda had been abused by her father when she was a child. Years later, after she was an

49. Mills, *This Little Light of Mine*, 307.
50. Canaan, "I Call Up Names," 81.

adult and married, she began attending a United Methodist church with a friend. Her life took on a new direction and a theological shift.

> Their [the United Methodist Church] theological stance was broadly based; their "God" was not so restrictive. And in this setting I again considered my personal relationship with God. This God loved me, just as I was; this God invited me to come to receive abundant life. . . . this new found relationship with God and a new community were too delightful to turn my back on.[51]

Linda's new relationship with God continued to mature. She eventually went to seminary and became a pastor. Her healing and self-transformation took several years of therapy and CPE (clinical pastoral education), but eventually she accepted the "gift of the grace of God." Her work, like that of Melba Wilson, now focuses on helping other women who have been abused.

Spirituality is an important component of moving beyond survival and embodying a transformative life of hope for Wilson. She commented:

> I had hoped that another more appropriate term than survivor, as a description of those of us who have made it "through the break," would present itself. None has emerged. It is important, though, at least to define what it is I mean when I say that we are more than survivors. One woman survivor said: "I want to thrive, not just survive. I am more than just a survivor. My life cannot simply be summed up as being a survivor."[52]

Moving beyond survival is linked to the unique spirituality of black women, which Wilson believes is distinct from the dominant culture's.

> As black women, I feel we have something very special about our lives. We bring something special to this dormant environment. We bring life to this place. . . . The spirituality of the majority of people in this environment is not a living one. It is not based on respect for life, courage, compassion or acceptance of others. It is not based on peace or friendship. . . . A lot of pain that black people experience has to do with their disconnection from their own spirituality. Everything to do with black people's spirituality has been denied and we have been taught not to feel it.[53]

Wilson primarily discusses abuse in the psychological model, yet she includes a brief section on spirituality. I think it is significant that, even from the psychotherapeutic model, the spiritual aspect of moving beyond survival is understood by Wilson as essential.

---

51. Hollies, "A Daughter Survives," 86.
52. Wilson, *Crossing the Boundary*, 194.
53. Ibid., 198.

Maya Angelou's life centers on two things: first, the rape and her subsequent muteness as a child, and second, her relationship with God. Her works are full of references to God's presence in her life. She links her ability to overcome abuse and to have hope in this life with the abiding presence of God. Cornel West interviewed her in his book, *Restoring Hope*, and she had the following response to his questions. When West asked her the sources of her hope and how we can talk about hope with so much suffering and pain the world today, Maya replied:

> In the worst of times, incredibly, that's when hope appears, like a seed, like a bulb splitting. One never knows what it cost a bulb to split, a lily or an onion, to split open. And that tendril to come out. But I do know that there's a song in the Genesis, there's a statement that it had rained so long, that people had given up the idea that the rain would cease. And then the Lord said that he would put a rainbow in the sky. There is that in Genesis. And in the nineteenth century, an African American wrote: "When it looked like the sun wasn't going to shine anymore, God put a rainbow in the clouds." Now that means that in the worst of times, in the dreariest of times, you can look into the clouds and see hope.[54]

Angelou uses the biblical symbol of the rainbow to talk about hope.

Hope has several metaphors for Angelou. For her, hope and courage go hand in hand. Courage involves the courage to *be* as well as the courage to "tell the truth about America in relation not just to white supremacy but to other forms of evil." For her, hope is also synonymous with love. "I believe," she says, "another word for hope is love." Love does not refer to "mush," sentimentality, or indulgence.[55] She relates this love as the kind of "against the odds love" her grandmother displayed to her after she was raped and became mute because she thought her words had the power to kill. After the murder of her rapist, Maya was sent to live with her grandmother.

> Mama (her grandmother) would braid my hair. I'd sit on the floor. She'd sit in the chair. . . . Mama would pull that brush in my hair. And she would say, "your Mama don't care what these people say about you, about you being a idiot or you being a moron because you can't talk. Mama know when the good Lord ready, you're going to be a preacher. Mama don't care what these people say, Sister. You just keep on reading that poetry. You just keep on

---

54. Cornel West, *Restoring Hope: Conversations on the Future of Black America* (Boston: Beacon Press, 1997), 189.
55. Ibid., 190–91.

being a good girl. You going to be somebody, Sister." I used to think, That poor ignorant woman. But here I am. That's love.[56]

It was this kind of love that kindled Angelou's passion for the possible in this life.

Absent from most of the other contemporary narratives that we have analyzed is the metaphorical biblical language that was found in the narratives of slavery and emancipation.[57] Wilson does use a birthing metaphor, the bringing of life, in her work, but she links it to a feminist, psychotherapeutic model rather than a biblical model. The most consistent theological theme in the selected contemporary narratives was the christocentric references. The earlier the narrative was written—that is, the closer to emancipation—the more heavily the theological language was employed. For example, Fannie Lou Hamer's narrative is as much theological as it is political. Her religious assertions and her political involvement were intertwined. Her passion for justice and transformation of the community was as much spiritual as social. As African American women obtained more "freedoms," such as the right to vote, desegregated education, and housing, the content of the narratives turned toward writing more intimately about healing the psychological pain of abuse, and only secondarily the theological disruption. The passion of life is focused on self-actualization, then community renewal through personal introspection, therapy, and a new appropriation of the gospel. In most cases, community renewal refers to assisting other abused women. It seems that as the context of abuse changed, the focus of hope narrowed. During slavery, abused women's passion was directed toward freedom for self from abuse but, to a larger degree, toward freedom for the community. The focus of hope during emancipation centered on voice, autonomy, and freedoms. The emancipation narratives contained more public concerns and less emphasis on the abuse that one had suffered. By the contemporary era, many of the external limiting facets of abuse of black women's bodies had been addressed, even if only to a limited degree. The Civil Rights Act of 1964 and affirmative action programs helped remove some of the sexist and racist barriers in American society. With resources available to, at least in theory, address the race, class, and gender oppression, black women began to write about the oppression from within their own communities and churches. Therefore, the contempo-

---

56. Ibid., 192.
57. See my discussions in chapters 2 and 3 of the use of biblical metaphors in the narratives. Sojourner likens herself to Esther; Old Elizabeth likens herself to Mary, the mother of Jesus, being "overshadowed with the Spirit"; Harriet Jacobs uses 1 Peter to describe her master as one who seeks to devour like Satan; Kate Drumgoold uses the Exodus motif; and Lucy Delaney uses Ephesians 5 to discuss her mother's fortitude.

rary narratives center on abuse from within the black community. Black women now had the opportunity to consider their own feelings and the impact of abuse on them spiritually and mentally. I am not suggesting that black women during slavery and emancipation were not self-aware, or did not struggle with the personal impact of abuse. Nor am I suggesting that contemporary African American women are not struggling with sociopolitical structures of oppression. I am suggesting that the context of abuse influenced the content of their narratives and the function of hope in their lives.

As we prepare to discuss the understanding of hope in the work of contemporary womanist theologians, we should keep in mind the hope of black women across the generations. It has changed focus, yet is still present. The theological undergirding was strongest during slavery and emancipation, yet it is still a vital component of black women's lives. All of the narratives include some reference to religious appropriations that empowered black women to seek life. Hope for slave women was a quest for full humanity and physical freedom. During emancipation, hope functioned to empower black women to seize public voice against the external inequities of life in America. As these inequities were addressed and equalized, at least in a limited sense through the civil rights movement, black women's narratives focused more acutely on the personal implications of abuse from within the black community. In each era hope has been theological, as well as sociopolitical. Activism has been coupled with faith. Hope has been a bridge for black women that moved them from oppression toward liberation, personally and communally. As we move to the next chapter, where we will look at womanist theologians' discussions of hope, a few questions loom large. Is the womanist theologians' understanding of hope consistent with or different from the bridge of hope that has been built by our foremothers? Humanity, voice, freedom, and equality were consistent themes in each era, to differing degrees. How are these themes reflected in the work of womanist theologians? Are the theological categories that womanist theologians have used to discuss hope consistent with the theological themes found in the narratives? And finally, how do these prolegomena move us closer to a womanist theology of hope from the voices of black women across the centuries?

Chapter 5

Womanist Visions

*H*aving analyzed the expressions of hope in selected narratives from slavery, emancipation, and the contemporary period, I am ready to bring these narratives into conversation with current discussions of hope in womanist theology. Hope has been a recurring theme in theology, in general, and is important to emergent womanist theology. The problem is that while hope has been widely written about in Western theology, and has been consistently expressed in black women's narratives, it has still to be adequately explored in womanist theology from the voices of African American women. Hope is frequently alluded to in womanist works, but a full exploration of the function of hope in the lives of African American women and its implications for womanist theology has not been developed.

This chapter brings the voices of abused black women into conversation with womanist theologians. As in the previous chapters, I go to the *voices* of these theologians. Karen Baker-Fletcher is a womanist theologian who has specifically written on the topic of hope in womanist theology. Her work on the subject is included in the first systematic treatment of womanist theology.[1] Brief treatments of black women's understanding of hope have been published in the works of Delores Williams and Jacquelyn Grant in the context of thematic treatments of womanist theology. Grant was one of the earliest womanist theologians[2] to begin to discuss black women's hope. She does so in her treatment of womanist Christology in her seminal work, *White*

---

1. Karen Baker-Fletcher and Garth KASIMU Baker-Fletcher, *My Sister, My Brother: Womanist and Xodus God-Talk* (Maryknoll, N.Y.: Orbis Books, 1997).
2. *Womanist theologian* is the designation for black women scholars writing theology from the perspective and experiences of black women. The designation was introduced by Jacquelyn Grant in 1989. See also chap. 1, n. 2.

Women's Christ and Black Women's Jesus.[3] Delores Williams's work in *Sisters in the Wilderness*[4] also touches on hope. She discusses hope through the biblical narrative and her treatment of the surrogate roles of black women in American society. Yet, Baker-Fletcher, Williams, and Grant have not gone to the narratives of black women to extract their understanding of hope and how hope functioned in their lives. Before we can discuss the impact of race, class, and gender on the oppression of black women's bodies, and black women's understanding of hope, one must listen, I assert, to the voices of black women. I have done this by going directly to their voices in their narratives.

This chapter draws together the results of the previous chapters to demonstrate how hope has been defined and how it has functioned in the lives of the abused African American women studied. The chapter draws out the threads of connectedness, that is, the similarities in nuances of hope, in the voices of abused African American women across the generations. It also discusses the dissimilarities that emerged as the contours of African American women's experience changed. The chapter concludes by articulating the contributions and limits of contemporary womanist theologians' discussions of hope in light of the material considered. The resulting information provides a foundation for articulating a contemporary womanist theology of hope.

In chapter 1 we began our discussion of hope with the work of womanist theologians Jacquelyn Grant, Delores Williams, and Karen Baker-Fletcher. We now return to their discussions of hope to bring them into conversation with the expressions of hope found in the narratives of victimized African American women from slavery, emancipation, and the contemporary periods.

Contemporary Womanist Theologians and Hope

The emergence of womanist theology is a contemporary movement. Womanist theology as an academic discipline began to take shape and evolved in the mid-1980s. Alice Walker's definition of *womanist* published in 1983 became the nomenclature for the work of many black scholars. Walker's definition emphasized the multigenerational character of African American women's lives, communal concerns, empowering vitality, spirituality, and

---

3. Jacquelyn Grant, *White Women's Christ and Black Women's Jesus: Feminist Christology and Womanist Response* (Atlanta: Scholars Press, 1989).
4. Delores Williams, *Sisters in the Wilderness: The Challenge of Womanist God-Talk* (Maryknoll, N.Y.: Orbis Books, 1993).

culture-sustaining elements.[5] Jacquelyn Grant was among the earliest African American theologians to name her work *womanist theology*. For Grant, womanist theologians engage in theology independent of white males or females and African American men. Womanists explore and construct theology through the lens of African American women's experience of multidimensional oppressions, such as racism, classism, sexism, and heterosexism.

Jacquelyn Grant

Both Jacquelyn Grant and Delores Williams have written extensively regarding the oppression of African American women during slavery, emancipation, and contemporary America. Grant discusses the abuse of black women's bodies during slavery, after emancipation, and today. She sets this discussion in the context of black women's understanding of Jesus and the central role that Jesus has always played in the lives of black women across the centuries. She asserts that black women have had to bear crosses of affliction that culminated in crucifixion, just like Jesus. "As Jesus was persecuted and made to suffer undeservedly, so were they (black women). His suffering culminated in the crucifixion. Their crucifixion included rape and babies being sold."[6] Black women's crucifixions have included having their families broken up when children were separated from parents, rapes, brutality, and the physical exploitation that black women have been forced to endure.

Grant also notes the physical exploitation of black women's bodies through manual labor. She adds that while all Christians are called to be servants like Jesus, black women have been more servant than any other group of people. She calls this the "sin of servanthood" that has been imposed on black women. This sin of servanthood has not only exploited black women through excessive physical labor, but has also demonstrated the classism under which black women live. Grant notes that the term *servant* has often been used

> . . . to relegate certain victimized people—those on the underside of history— to the lower rungs of society. Consequently, politically disenfranchised peoples have generally been perceived as the servants class of the politically powerful. Nonwhite peoples, it is believed by many white people, were created for the primary purpose of providing service for white people. Likewise in patriarchal societies, the notions of service and servant were often used to describe the role women played in relation to men and children.

---

5. See Walker's complete definition of *womanist* in Alice Walker, *In Search of Our Mothers' Garden: Womanist Prose* (San Diego: Harcourt Brace Jovanovich, 1983), xi–xii.

6. Grant, *White Women's Christ and Black Women's Jesus*, 212.

Black women's reality reveals that they are further removed from the top-side of history. In fact, African American women have been the "servants of servants."[7] The sin of servanthood confined many black women to jobs without pay during slavery, and low-paying jobs, often in the domestic service industry, after emancipation. For Grant, this raises the theological issue of theodicy in relation to black women because black women's service has usually meant a life of suffering.

Grant discusses the brutality that black women have suffered at the hands of white women and black men across the centuries. For instance, she writes:

> Brutality was administered not only by masters and foremen but also by mistresses, reflecting the fact that White women were just as much participants in the system as were White men. For every Angelina and Sarah Grimke there were numerous of those like their mother who not only condoned slavery but thought that abolitionists like Angelina and Sarah were agitators, if not in fact heretics.[8]

Emancipation was "slavery without chains" and did little to change the condition of black women or the *image* of black people as inferior beings meant for servanthood. Significant to Grant's discussion of the abuse of black women's bodies is "how black women's experience involves a convergence of racism, sexism, and classism."[9] These "isms" underline the oppression of black women by white men and women, and black men. Grant asserts that even after slavery the servanthood motif was perpetuated. She asserts that the "physical brutality toward blacks was continued, and even extended outside the work place. The immediate relationship between white women and black women did not change; white women were still the oppressors and black women were still oppressed . . . black women were still treated as property."[10] Poor black women continued to be "more servant than anyone else" in American society because of their gender, race, and class. This abuse was meted out by white men and women, and to some degree by black men.

Grant was among the earliest womanist theologians to challenge the black church and the theological academy on its spiritual and physical abuse of

---

7. Jacquelyn Grant, "The Sin of Servanthood and the Deliverance of Discipleship," in *A Troubling in My Soul: Womanist Perspectives on Evil and Suffering*, ed. Emilie Townes (Maryknoll, N.Y.: Orbis Books, 1993), 200.

8. Grant, *White Women's Christ and Black Women's Jesus*, 197.

9. Ibid., 198.

10. Ibid.

black women.[11] Grant critiqued James Cone's early works, as well as that of other early black liberation theologians, as sexist and overlooking the contributions of black women to the black church, academy, and society. She cautioned black liberation theologians not to overlook the racism from the dominant society as well as the sexism of the black community under which black women live.[12]

Grant has also written articles about contemporary black women who were empowered to overcome abusive situations. Her work includes articles on the lives of Sojourner Truth[13] and Fannie Lou Hamer[14] as examples of black women empowered by God to overcome victimization and facilitate communal transformation. Grant, like Sojourner and Fannie Lou, refused to be silenced regarding the oppression of black women.

Delores Williams

Delores Williams discusses the abuse of black women's bodies through the biblical narratives of Hagar, a slave woman of African heritage, whose body was exploited at the whim of her mistress and master.[15] Williams argues that "Genesis 16:1–16 illustrates what the history of many African American women taught them long ago; that is, the slave woman's story is unavoidably shaped by the problems and desires of her master."[16] Williams likens the sexual surrogate role of Hagar to the surrogate roles black women across the centuries have been forced to fulfill. Williams likens the lack of control Hagar had over her body, and her life of limited resources for survival, to the brutalization of black women's bodies from slavery through the contemporary era. She also notes the limited resources for survival that have been afforded to black women. The alienation and sense of being an outsider that were a part of Hagar's experience have also been the experience of black women, according to Williams. Just as God participated in the survival of Hagar and her child, God participated in the survival of black women and their children. But

---

11. Grant does an extensive critique of literature written by black women exposing the abuse they have suffered in the church. See her discussion in *White Women's Christ and Black Women's Jesus*, 206–209.

12. See Jacquelyn Grant, "Black Women and Black Theology," in *Black Theology: A Documentary History, 1966–1979*, ed. Gayraud S. Wilmore and James H. Cone (Maryknoll, N.Y.: Orbis Books 1979), 418–33.

13. See Jacquelyn Grant, "A Refusal to Be Silenced," in *Sojourners* (December 1986): 23–24.

14. Cf. Jacquelyn Grant, "Civil Rights Women: A Source for Doing Womanist Theology," in *Black Women in the Civil Rights Movement: Trailblazers and Torchbearers, 1941–1965*, ed. Vicki L. Crawford, Jacqueline Anne Rouse, and Barbara Woods (Bloomington: Indiana University Press, 1990), 39–49.

15. See Genesis, chaps. 16 and 21.

16. Williams, *Sisters in the Wilderness*, 15.

part of survival and overcoming oppression was human initiative. God prompted Hagar to see and use resources she was unaware she had. Hagar, asserts Williams, "becomes the first female in the Bible to liberate herself from oppressive power structures."[17] This same divine empowerment and human initiative is found in the lives of black women such as Harriet Jacobs, Sojourner Truth, and Fannie Lou Hamer.

Williams's discussion of the forced surrogacy of black women's bodies is one of the most extensive theological discussions of the abuse of black women's bodies by a womanist theologian. Williams uses varied and rich sources for her work. Yet, she uses the narratives of black women minimally. She alludes to black women's hope in the book, but her primary discussion centers around the biblical narratives of Genesis 16 and 21 regarding Hagar. Hagar, for Williams, embodies the passion for humanity, voice, and autonomy that characterizes black women's hope.

For Williams, it is also Jesus' "life of resistance" and "survival strategies" that foster hope.[18] She couches this discussion in her treatment of surrogacy and redemption. Given the historic legacy of abuse of African American women's bodies, Williams challenges the validity of the symbolism of the cross as an emblem of salvation. Williams questions the value put on sacrifice and suffering in Christian religion.[19] She asserts that the image of an innocent person's death as the vehicle of salvation is a destructive model for African American women, who have, in many instances, been forced to serve as surrogates. She says that black women have to bear the cross of rearing children without help, dealing with inadequate health care, poverty, and violence, as well as the crosses of racism and sexism.[20] If Jesus died for humanity then, for Williams, he was the ultimate surrogate—whether voluntary or coerced. She asserts that it was not his surrogate death that was salvific. Rather, salvation came through his life, which demonstrated resistance and the survival strategies. It was Jesus' life that negated the death of identity and lack of personhood suffered by the outcast of humanity.[21] The death of identity occurred with the social and cultural dislocation of African women and men brought to America and enslaved. A sociopolitical understanding of Jesus' salvific value "frees redemption from the cross and frees the cross from

---

17. Ibid., 19.
18. Ibid., 164–66.
19. Delores Williams, "African American Women Develop a New Theological Vision in the Ecumenical Decade: Churches in Solidarity with Women," in *The Brown Papers*, vol. 1 (Boston: Women's Theological Center Press, 1994).
20. Williams, *Sisters in the Wilderness*, 169.
21. Ibid., 164.

the sacred aura put around it by existing patriarchal responses to the question of which Jesus' death represents."[22] Williams asserts that Jesus conquered sin through his living, not through his dying. For Williams, the substitutionary atonement is an affirmation of sexual surrogate roles black women have been forced to fulfill in America. It also validates child abuse (a parent sacrificing a child on a cross) and other forms of violence against women and children in society. Williams sums up her position by adding "[a]s Christians, Black women cannot forget the cross, but neither can they glorify it. To do so is to glorify suffering and to render their exploitation sacred. To do so is to glorify the sin of defilement."[23] Hope, then, for African American women is found in the liberated struggle for a quality of life in harmony with God's vision for humanity. Williams states that the "kingdom of God is a metaphor for hope God gives those attempting to right the relations between self and self, between self and others, between self and God."[24] The passion of life comes through emulating the model of Jesus' life and vision here on earth. Jesus' life demonstrated his willingness to be present in the struggles of the oppressed. Black women's hope, Williams asserts, is fostered by their belief that Jesus is involved in their daily struggles.[25]

While Grant and Williams allude to black women's understanding of hope, neither has written on what black women express in their narratives as hope. Their discussions of hope are set in the context of thematic discussions of womanist theology. Grant uses Christology to discuss hope. The conditions under which African Americans are forced to live, even today, are the cross of Jesus. Yet black women understood that there was more to life than daily crosses. There was also the resurrection. Grant asserts, "the resurrection brings the hope that liberation is immanent." She explains that the resurrected Black Christ signifies this hope for the lives of black women.[26] The resurrection, for Grant, signifies that the multidimensional oppression of black women is only the *context* in which they experience hope and liberation. Jesus suffers along with the abused of society. He identifies with the marginalized of society—that is, black women—affirms their humanity, and inspires active hope.[27] Active hope means, for Grant, that black women are involved in their own liberation. Their faith empowers them to become participants in sociopolitical change for the betterment of their own lives and that of their commu-

---

22. Ibid.
23. Ibid., 167.
24. Ibid., 166.
25. Ibid., 203.
26. Grant, *White Women's Christ and Black Women's Jesus*, 216.
27. Ibid., 216–17. See also 209–18.

nity. Religion is not an opiate that lulls them into a sense of complacency to wait for liberation in the sweet by and by. African American women are active subjects of liberation, the transformative agents of hope through their relationship with Jesus. Jesus, "the divine co-sufferer," empowers black women to access their passion for the possible in this life. Jesus identifies so readily with the struggles of black women, and is so present in their liberation, that "this Christ, found in the experiences of Black women, is a Black woman."[28]

Karen Baker-Fletcher

Karen Baker-Fletcher discusses hope in the traditional Western theological category of eschatology. Baker-Fletcher is the first womanist theologian, to my knowledge, to develop a systematic treatment of womanist theology. Grant's work has focused primarily on Christology and black women's understanding of Jesus. She relates this very closely to the power of language and the oppression of black women in the church, academy, and society. Williams's work has centered around the abuse of black women's bodies through a dialogue with the biblical narratives on Hagar. Her application of the implications of her work for the contemporary womanist centers also primarily on how the appropriation of patriarchal Western religious symbols and language affect black women in the church as well as in society. Neither Grant nor Williams has discussed hope as a theological category as Baker-Fletcher has done in her systematic treatment of womanist theology. As do black liberation and feminist theologians, Baker-Fletcher understands hope as eschatological. Her eschatology is primarily focused on transformation of the current condition of the world. For Baker-Fletcher, hope involves the transformation of both humanity and creation to experience the kingdom of God, on earth and in heaven, which is at hand.

Like Williams, she focuses on a specific biblical passage to discuss hope. She references Psalm 27 as a passage that "speaks of eschatological hope and promise in God as the strength of life who sustains not only one's self but the universe."[29] She notes that for the womanist, eschatology is not purely concerned with last things or end-time occurrences. For Baker-Fletcher, eschatological hope and envisionment informs the "daily moment-by-moment business of living."[30]

---

28. Ibid., 220.
29. Baker-Fletcher, *My Sister, My Brother*, 286.
30. Ibid.

Baker-Fletcher also goes to the life of Anna Julia Cooper to nuance womanist hope. Cooper's life (1858–1964) spans the nineteenth and twentieth centuries. She was born in slavery and lived through the civil rights era. Cooper was proud of the achievements of black people in a hostile country and an advocate of women's rights, particularly black women. For Cooper, the "hereafter" was so close that "we must live into it."[31] Baker-Fletcher points out that hope for Cooper was not a matter of a "sweet by-and-by" concept of God's justice but was a transformative social gospel lived by black women and men.

Baker-Fletcher begins her exploration of Cooper's life with the theme of the possibilities of a contemporary womanist theology of hope looming large. She asks, "How does one go about the task of constructing a theology of hope in a time when optimism is questioned? . . . If they [African Americans] found hope for freedom and equality in the midst of slavery and Jim Crow, surely hope is possible today. . . . Only by remembering who one is and to whom one belongs can there be a revival of hope."[32] Though Baker-Fletcher begins with a question regarding a theology hope for today, her focus from Cooper's life is the God presence, "the Singing Something" that pervades Cooper's quest for voice. Baker-Fletcher's primary treatment of Cooper's life revolves around her quest for voice in an era that sought to silence the voice of black women. She also explores the theological themes in Cooper's life and reads her narrative as a theological text. Baker-Fletcher's primary treatment of hope occurs in her systematic development of womanist theology.

Other Womanist Voices

Recent work in womanist theology continues to nuance hope. While it is common to find some reference to hope in most womanist works, two excellent examples can be noted in Emilie Townes and Diana Hayes, who explore hope in their most recent works.[33] Townes identifies hope as paradoxical in nature. While we must hope, we are afraid to hope. Hope is full of possibilities and yet brimming with dangers. Hope interrupts the mundane and the comfortable while protesting prophetic fury. Hope is that which scares us and yet prepares us to confront the atrocities of life. Townes challenges us to breathe new life

---

31. Ibid., 287.

32. Karen Baker-Fletcher, *A Singing Something: Womanist Reflections on Anna Julia Cooper* (New York: Crossroad Publishing Co., 1994), 28–29.

33. Townes began her exploration of hope in an earlier work, *Womanist Justice: Womanist Hope* (Atlanta: Scholars Press, 1993). Her development and explication of hope comes to maturity in *Embracing the Spirit: Womanist Perspectives on Hope, Salvation, and Transformation* (Maryknoll, N.Y.: Orbis Books, 1997).

into dying hopes. Hope, for Townes, usually emerges out of communal and personal lament. This courage out of lament is grounded in the risen Christ, who provides a firm foundation for engaging life free of the shackles of modern oppressions. Hope empowers us to keep on keeping on, even in the face of disappointment. It gives us strength and yet exposes us to vulnerability. Hope charges us to risk something for the sake of transformed life for ourselves and our communities. Hope refuses to acquiesce to the status quo or powers that be by answering life with life.[34]

Diana Hayes explores hope in the face of contemporary violence in Los Angeles after the Rodney King verdict. Violence is more than overt acts such as rape, beatings, hanging, shooting, and stabbing. Violence is violation of one's personhood, an assault on human dignity, and a denial that one is created in the image of God. It is the "thingification" or "objectification" of persons. A basic form of violence is the sociopolitical structures that institutionalize injustices. This systemic violence often erupts in revolt (by the oppressed) or repression (by the oppressor). Hayes calls on Christians to instill faith and to be the bearers of hope in today's spiraling world of injustices. Our spirituality is the grounding force that prevents the reeling of this world from overtaking us.

Hope demands that we return to love. The failure to love ourselves and one another has led to "spiritual impoverishment that threatens the very structure of our church and society." Love heals inner wounds, stops pity parties, and aids black women and men to nonviolently confront oppression and to persist regardless. Our task is to "gather the scattered threads of our history" and to weave them into a tapestry of our future.[35]

Threads of Connectedness across the Centuries

In the previous chapter, I argued that there were some consistent elements in black women's narratives that can be brought into conversation with current discussions of hope in womanist theology. The narratives of slavery, emancipation, and the contemporary era have several connecting cords. The distinctive *enormous*, *transgenerational*, and *maldistributed* character of hope permeates the narratives of each era, as well as the work of womanist

---

34. Townes, "The Doctor Ain't Taking No Sticks" in *Embracing the Spirit: Womanist Perspectives on Hope, Salvation, and Transformation*. Several of the articles in this volume, particularly in part 1, explore nuances of hope.

35. Diana Hayes, "My Hope Is in the Lord" in Townes, *Embracing the Spirit*, 9–27.

theologians. Black women across the generations "hoped against hope" in the midst of contexts that were both dehumanizing and disempowering. The enormity of their ability to hope was demonstrated in their unrelenting determination to cling to a modicum of dignity in the face of degradation. Harriet Jacobs held on to her hope and hid for seven years from her master. Lucy Delaney's life was "thorns in plenty with no roses," yet she was willing to give her life that black women, as well as other oppressed persons, could obtain an education. Though abused by a father who was also a minister, Linda Hollies's passion for life enabled her to eventually become a pastor whose ministry focuses on assisting abused African American women to thrive in the church and the community. In spite of personal experiences that were abusive and dehumanizing, these women fought for full humanity for themselves and others.

African American women were empowered by the *transgenerational* faith and activism instilled in them by family and friends. Their sense of personal empowerment, which was both spiritual and communal, was lived in their sociopolitical and spiritual lives. They inculcated a passion for the possible in this life into their children and community. Hope transcended contextual eras and was handed on from generation to generation. The passion and power of black foremothers was the conduit through which contemporary African American women gleaned the impetus to hope in spite of victimization from within, as well as outside, the African American community.

African American women, whether slaves or free, have been actuated by the *maldistributed* hope expressed in their lives. Gender inequities have made them the servants of servants, and the least of the "least of them." Multidimensional oppressions have been molded into multifocal engagement of society and the church, black cultural appropriations, and black religious sensibilities in the academy as well as outside it.

As we attempt to discern the threads of connectedness between African American women's narratives and womanist theology, we must return to an earlier question. Is the discussion of hope by womanist theologians consistent with the hope embedded in the selected African American women's narratives?

It must be noted that womanist theology as an academic discipline is in its infancy. Its birth as an academic discipline only dates back to the mid-1980s. Thus, there are multiple themes and issues that are yet to be explored by womanist theologians. This includes the theme of hope in black women's narratives. Womanist theologians have begun to discuss hope in their work, yet there is much more critical exploration to be done. Grant, Williams, and Baker-Fletcher nuance hope in each of their works. Its engagement has been parenthetical to other thematic presentations, but is nonetheless present.

Grant clearly reflects on the *enormity* and *maldistributed* nature of African American women's hope. She notes that the literature of black women, including their narratives and literary works, lays the historical foundation on which first-, second-, and third-generation womanist scholars can derive black women's religious sensibilities. These religious sensibilities undergird black women's understanding of Christ, who empowers an active hope in their lives. This means that black women across the centuries have anchored their hope in the resurrected Christ rather than whites (male or female) or males (black or white). Grant notes that "black women's affirmation of Jesus as God meant that White people were not God."[36] In her discussion of Jesus' empowering presence in the lives of black women, Grant goes briefly to the narratives of slave women like Sojourner Truth to give voice to the kind of tenacious love that empowered black people to continually fight for freedom.[37] Grant's work places strong emphasis on the enormity and maldistributed character of black women's hope as they were empowered by "Jesus as God" in their lives.

The selected womanist theologians have all noted the *transgenerational* character of abuse, as well as black women's empowered passion for humanity, voice, and equality in this life. Through her discussion of Hagar, Williams draws out the striking parallels between the oppression and the empowerment of Hagar, and the experiences of African American women across the centuries. Even today, she notes, "most of Hagar's situation is congruent with many African American women's predicament of poverty, sexual and economic exploitation, surrogacy, domestic violence, homelessness, rape, motherhood, single parenting, ethnicity and meeting with God."[38] Just as God empowered Hagar to survive oppression, Williams notes God's empowerment of black women today. Hagar is symbolic of the hope that has been infused into the community across the generations. The Hagar symbolism "held together women's and the community's past history, present situations and intimations of hope for a better future."[39] Hope for Williams is the promise of survival and a quality of life that resists abuse. This resistance and survival posture is made possible to all generations of black women through Jesus' life of resistance, and resurrected presence in their lives. It is the "uncanny resilience" says Williams, of the "mothering/nurturing/caring/enduring and resistance capacities of Hagar and Black women [that] has

---

36. Grant, *White Women's Christ and Black Women's Jesus*, 213.
37. Ibid., 214.
38. Williams, *Sisters in the Wilderness*, 5–6.
39. Ibid., 118.

birthed a spirit of hope in the community."[40] This spirit of hope is forged in the spirituality and politics of black women and fosters resistance for them, their communities, and future generations.

Another similarity in African American women's personal narratives and the discussion of hope by womanist theologians is the communal dimension of hope. Though for the most part womanist theologians have not explicitly explored a womanist theology of hope directly from the voices of black women, they do consistently resist notions of individualism. This tendency to speak of the communal character of African American women's spirituality explicates the communal nature of hope found in the narratives of slave, emancipated, and contemporary women. Walker's definition of *womanist* uplifts its inclusive, communal nature. Walker says "a womanist is committed to the survival and wholeness of entire people, male and female. . . . Is traditionally capable as in: Mamma, I'm walking to Canada and I'm taking you and a bunch of other slaves with me."[41] Thus the communal dimensions of African American women's hope has been penned in their narratives, as well as by black feminists, black liberation theologians, Walker, and womanist theologians.

Of greater significance is the fact that the women in the selected narratives, as well as contemporary womanist theologians, have consistently noted the this-worldly focus of African American women's hope. Hope for black women has both ultimate and penultimate expression, but black women's passion for the possible centers on spiritual and sociopolitical activism in this life. Karen Baker-Fletcher reiterates her understanding of the "Reign of God which is at hand" in her dialogue with her husband, black liberation theologian Garth KASIMU Baker-Fletcher. KASIMU Baker-Fletcher understands African Americans' hope as a revolutionary NOW hope that is a series of choices and decisions that are ongoing day to day to facilitate psychospiritual health and healing in this life. Karen Baker-Fletcher cautions that one must be aware of the promise and the problems of working to bring about the vision of revolutionary NOW hope of the reign of God on earth. She notes:

> Visions are both powerful and fragile. They can be insightful or misleading, depending on the vision and how it is interpreted. Whether the kingdom of God is envisioned in this life or the next, the results of the vision can be helpful or dangerous, depending on the level of discernment, testing, and accountability to others. . . . There are instances where visions of the Kingdom of God are more profane and violent than they first appear to those who believe in them and feel included in them. Theological visions,

---

40. Ibid., 235.
41. Walker, *In Search of Our Mothers' Garden*, xi.

for example, that blame the poor for their own poverty, assuming it is the result of sin, are problematic. Racialized notions of slave owners' spiritual superiority to their slaves and the rightfulness of their ownership of people of darker hue are equally problematic.[42]

Baker-Fletcher asserts that womanist scholars, like Emilie Townes, have noted that living in hope fosters a just society now. For Townes, womanist hope engenders "a society that is uncompromisingly rooted in justice and fueled by people who use their hope to construct and enact meaningful and significant social change."[43] Hope is, says Karen Baker-Fletcher, "not only in the future. Hope is present and in history as each moment lived in faith moves from future to present time and past time."[44] While hope does expect fulfillment in the ultimate expression of God's kingdom, for black women and womanist theologians hope is primarily concerned with this world.

The most consistent similarity between the selected narratives and the discussion of womanist theologians' discussion of hope is hope's christocentric center. In the face of victimization or valor, Jesus Christ is the empowering force in the lives of African American women. It was Jesus who made possible the counter-cultural appropriation of religion for Sojourner Truth. For Truth there was a "religion of America" and the "religion of Jesus." The religion of Jesus prompted Sojourner to fight for women's rights. Fannie Lou Hamer's activism rested on her understanding of Jesus as a militant Messiah who was involved with "grass root people" in the alleviation of oppression. Jacquelyn Grant's discussion of hope is set in her discussion of Jesus' empowering presence in the lives of black women. After Grant's discussion of Jesus as the one who inspires active hope in the lives of black women, she references the voice of a slave woman whose prayer elucidates the centrality of Jesus to the hope of black women. The slave prayed:

Dear Massa Jesus, we all uns beg Ooner [you] come make us a call dis yere day. We is nutting but poor Ethiopian women and people ain't tink much 'bout we. We ain't trust any od dem great high people to come to we church, but do' yu is the one great Massa, great too much dan Massa Linkum, you ain't shame to care for we African people.[45]

For Delores Williams, the discussion of hope centers around Jesus' life of resistance and the symbolism his death on the cross communicates for those

---

42. Karen Baker-Fletcher, *My Sister, My Brother,* 283–84.
43. Emilie Townes, "Living in the New Jerusalem," in *A Troubling in My Soul,* 89.
44. Baker-Fletcher, *My Sister, My Brother,* 291.
45. Harold Carter, *The Prayer Tradition of Black People* (Valley Forge, Pa.: Judson Press, 1976), 49.

who have been abused and victimized. Williams uses the biblical metaphor of Hagar to talk about black women's experiences, but her appropriation of the hope-filled possibilities for black women's lives is centered in Jesus. For Williams, the resurrection of Jesus and the kingdom of God are metaphors of hope that provide black women with the knowledge of abundant, fully human living. Abundant living in Jesus, which Williams calls his ministerial vision, fosters peaceful, productive relationships among body, mind, and spirit. Humanity, says Williams, is "redeemed through Jesus' ministerial vision of life."[46]

While many threads of connectedness exist between the expressions of hope in the selected narratives and the discussions of hope in contemporary womanist theology, there are also some dissimilarities that emerge out of the contours of the womanist textual analysis.

Dissimilarities of the Various Contexts

A significant dissimilarity in the narratives is the expression or focus of hope in the various eras. During slavery, black women's hope focused on obtaining freedom and humane treatment. The passion for life meant first of all being treated as human with the right to control one's life and make choices about one's body. Once slavery ended, emancipated black women wanted "voice." They wanted to reveal their experiences, express their views, and be heard by a wider audience. They did this by publishing their narratives and recounting the horrors of slavery. The contemporary expressions of hope in black women's narratives centered around autonomy and equality inside the black community as well as the larger society. The contemporary narratives reveal the personal intimate struggles of self-validation when victimization comes from within the black community and from outside, as well as from inside the black church and from the society. All of these nuances are present, to some degree, in each era (especially the quest to be treated as full humanity). Yet, the major focus of hope shifted as the contours of African American women's oppression changed.

Womanist theologians have not discussed the focus of hope in their writings. Humanity, voice, freedom, and equality are general threads that are referenced in the work of contemporary womanist theologians, but generally, these foci have not been specifically explicated in relation to hope and African

---

46. Williams, *Sisters in the Wilderness*, 167.

American women. Karen Baker-Fletcher begins her book on the life of Anna Julia Cooper by discussing hope in Cooper's life, but the theme is not carried through her work. She opens her book by asking how it is possible to construct a theology of hope in a society in which "the virus of nihilism at work in Black America afflicts both spiritual and socio-economic well being."[47] She alludes to the need for a theology of hope but shifts her attention to her area of interest—the God presence in Cooper's life.

Baker-Fletcher returns to Cooper's life in her systematic discussion of hope as eschatological. She explores Cooper's understanding of Jesus, which is hope filled and eschatological. Cooper's understanding of Jesus in relation to eschatology, asserts Baker-Fletcher, "speaks to the ministerial empowerment of Black women."[48] She sees this empowerment in two ways. First, "just as black mothers are vital elements in the regeneration of a particular race, Jesus is the vital element in the regeneration of civilization."[49] And second, she notes that present generations have hope for the future because of the legacy left in the past. For Baker-Fletcher this refers to black women, as well as to Jesus.[50]

In her systematic treatment of hope as eschatology, Baker-Fletcher also emphasizes hope in terms of its import for humanity and nature. Respect for the body of women is directly related to respect for the integrity of nature. She develops a christocentric eco-womanism that has Jesus as its center, and at the same time demands abundant life for black women, society in general, and nature. For her, the ultimate and eternal aim of hope is the healing and wholeness of all creation.[51] The narratives and the work of other womanists have put little focus on ecological justice. Of course, with the continued abuse of nature over the centuries, the issue of environmental integrity is a contemporary problem that has come to the fore. The cry for care of nature was overshadowed by the quest for fully human life.

Other than Williams's discussion of Hagar, the biblical metaphorical language that was so prevalent in the narratives of slavery and emancipation is absent from womanist theologians' discussions of hope. And, even though Williams sees many parallels in the life of Hagar and the plight of African American women, she does not wholeheartedly embrace Hagar as a model of a liberated human being. She acknowledges her initiative, hope, and empowerment but adds that Hagar, like African American women, had limited control

---

47. Baker-Fletcher, *A Singing Something*, 28.
48. Baker-Fletcher, *My Sister, My Brother*, 291.
49. Ibid.
50. Ibid.
51. Ibid., 292–98.

over her body and circumstances because of the power structure of the dominant culture. Though Hagar, to a limited extent, liberated herself from the power
structure, Williams does not view her as a model of fully human existence.
Womanist theology, notes Williams, "would be reticent to designate either
Hagar or the Virgin Mary as models of liberated human beings since both
women are always powerless and never able to take care of *their own* business
or set *their own agenda* for their lives."[52] Thus, while Williams sees some parallels in the life of Hagar and African American women, she understands Hagar
as a limited model at best. Slave and emancipated women who used biblical
metaphors tended to understand biblical women as models of their lives and
relationship with God; for example, Sojourner Truth called herself Esther
because, like Esther, she demanded an audience with the persons in power to
speak on behalf of her people to gain their freedom; Old Elizabeth likened herself to Mary, who was "overshadowed by the Holy Spirit."

Womanist theologians more often turn to historical black women, such as
Sojourner Truth, and to contemporary literature—for example, the work of
Alice Walker and Toni Morrison—to talk about the abuse of black women's
bodies as well as their empowerment and transformative presence in the black
community. The use of fictional literature that accurately reflects the trials and
triumphs of African American women has grown increasingly popular since
the advent of womanist theology as an academic discipline. Katie Cannon was
among the earliest to write about the adequacy of using the literature of black
women as a theological source.[53] It is from this literary repository that womanist theologians have drawn their metaphors. Baker-Fletcher speaks of God
as a "Singing Something" from the work of Anna Julia Cooper. The "Singing
Something" is the voice of God "that rises up within humanity in every nation
to cry out against injustice."[54] For Baker-Fletcher, this means that humans are
not only created in the image of God, but also in the voice of God. The
"Singing Something" is the "Divine spark" or "urge cell" that empowers
African American women for transformative activism. Grant was one of the
early scholars who turned to the work of Alice Walker as a reflection of the
struggles and strengths of African American women. Grant notes that
Walker's novel, *The Color Purple*, makes clear the racist oppression black
women face in a white society and the sexist oppression black women experience in the black community. Walker asserts "that the experience of being a
black woman or a white woman is so different that another word is required

---

52. Williams, *Sisters in the Wilderness*, 182.
53. See the Introduction to Katie Cannon, *Black Womanist Ethics* (Atlanta: Scholars Press, 1988).
54. Baker-Fletcher, *A Singing Something*, 16.

to describe the liberative efforts of black women."[55] Walker suggests that *womanist*, derived from the word *womanish* in black women's culture, is a more appropriate naming.[56] Rather than biblical metaphorical self-naming, womanist theologians turn to historical and literary works as a reflection of the hope and transformative agency of African American women.

This chapter demonstrates that womanist theologians have held onto the thread of Hope in black women narratives. Contemporary narratives and womanist thematic explorations share the distinctive character of hope found in slave and emancipation narratives. Hope in the voices of twentieth-century black women is multifocal: Hope is the promise of survival and quality of life (Williams), a revolutionary force that is this-worldly (Baker-Fletcher), and is anchored in Jesus and the kingdom of God (Grant, Williams, Baker-Fletcher). The similarities and dissimilarities between the selected narratives and the work of womanist theologians provide the foundation for discussing the contributions and limits of womanist theology as prolegomena to a womanist theology of hope.

---

55. Grant, *White Women's Christ and Black Women's Jesus*, 204.
56. Ibid., 203.

Conclusion:
Emergent Hope in Womanist Theology

*T*his study is important because it shows several important developments in black women's narratives, womanist thought, and theology in general. First, womanist understandings of hope, while consistent with the bridge of hope from black foremothers, is swinging back and forth in theological winds. This bridge of hope must be anchored in the voices of black women. Second, hope is clearly theological, not just psychosocial. Hope is anchored in the Lord. Hope is actualized in this world, as well as in the life to come. Third, the theological categories used to discuss hope must be enlarged to include the "Jesus theology," "Immanuel theology," and "Hope in the Holler theology" found in the narratives of black women. Fourth, there are critical implications for the black church. The transformative power of the black church has been weakened by the eroticism of affluence, education, and "opportunity." Last, humanity needs a hope that is particular yet not exclusive: hope that elucidates the plight of black women (men and children) but does not forget the oppression of other peoples. The Holler of terrorism, nihilism, resurgent racism, and economic instability suggest that a Hope, grounded in the Lord, is appropriate and necessary. In the wake of September 11, Americans, black, white, red, yellow, and brown, have resurrected the slogan "Keep hope alive." Our souls cry for Hope in the midst of our contemporary Holler.

I have explored the contours of hope across the generations. What sets this study apart is the fact that I have gone to the *voices* of black women through their narratives. The womanist textual analysis substantiates that changes in the sociopolitical context, and its attendant forms of oppression, influence the content of the narratives. In the content of the narrative, like an ancient Phoenix, a distinctive theology of hope emerges from the ashes of oppression. Black women's hope empowers them personally, as well as communally, in each era and connects them across generations.

The hope that emerges in the echos of the Holler during slavery is the quest for *freedom* and *humanity*. We explored the narratives of slavery as the foundational genre out of which black women's hope can be gleaned. The narratives of slave women elucidate the dehumanizing horrors and the distinctive hopes of life during de jure slavery. Hope, the passion for the possible in their lives, was expressed by slave women as an undauntable seizing of life in spite of abuse. Slave women lived in the daily personal humiliation of the Holler. Their bodies and being were disregarded, disrespected, and despised.

Yet in the midst of their oppression, black women were empowered by their faith. They differentiated between the religion of the slave master and the religion of Jesus. Jesus was the hermeneutical key for interpreting their relationship with God and others. Slaves lived a radical incarnational "Jesus theology." They found in "their Jesus" an Almighty friend who affirmed their humanity, empowered them to speak against injustices, and enabled them to experience freedom in the thrall of bondage. Jesus understood their struggles and gave them the power to bear their daily crosses of life. Their faith, the religion of Jesus, undergirded slave women's passion for the possible in this life, not just the life to come.

The seizing of hope contained in the slave narratives is reflected and expanded during emancipation and reconstruction and through urbanization. Black women raised their voices to tell their own personal struggles and at the same time lived in hope. The ex-slave interviews of the 1930s gave voice to over one thousand women whose horrors and hopes would have otherwise died with them. Combined with the book-length autobiographical narratives that emerged during this period, black women seized *public voice* in a sociohistorical context that sought to silence and control them. The content of the narratives shifts from personal atrocities to public activism.

Religion played a central role in black women's ability to express and live into hope during emancipation. The counter-cultural appropriation of religion seen in the slave narratives takes a different nuance in the emancipation narratives. The "presence of God" enabled emancipated black women to actualize their faith. This "Immanuel theology" permeates the narratives during this period. Jesus was most frequently referenced in connection with their *conversion*, while God with them was their source of empowerment in the "crying times." The metaphorical use of biblical language was also a vehicle for expressing the hope and empowerment of black women during emancipation. Black women likened their lives and mission to bold biblical characters, such as Mary the mother of Jesus, Esther, and Moses. Black women, girded up by their faith in God, love of community, and commitment to the black church, seized public voice on behalf of the marginalized of American society.

The contemporary period saw an even greater shift in the focus of hope and the content of the narratives. As external oppressions were addressed, the narratives focused on oppression *within*, as well as outside, the black community. The contemporary narratives explore the psychological effects and the theological disruption of abuse of being "wounded in the house of a friend."[1] The quest for *autonomy* and *equality* inside the community as well as the larger society is salient in the contemporary narratives. The religious themes in the slavery and emancipation narratives are present, but in a weaker voice. The contemporary narratives contain a "Hope in the Holler theology." The Holler stems from within the community, the church, and often, one's own home. Yet hope remains the bridge that empowers black women to move from situations of oppression to life-giving transformative possibilities. The oppression of each period was undergirded by its particular social myths that were used, and to a large extent are still being used, to justify the abuse and dehumanization of black women. Overarching each period is a hope that is enormous, transgenerational, and maldistributed. The threads of hope in each generation beg to be woven together into a tapestry of a womanist theology of hope.

Womanist theologians have began to explore hope but have not gone to the voices of black women. Nuances of hope are present in work of Grant, Williams, and Baker-Fletcher and the more recent works of Townes and Hayes. Because hope is a consistent and pivotal theme, from slavery through contemporary womanist theologians' work, one would expect to see a stronger development of a theology of hope. Perhaps one could postulate that womanist theologians have not written a theology of hope because womanist theology is a nascent theology and needs additional research and responses to the area of hope.

The references to hope found in the narratives and the work of womanist theologians suggest that a womanist theology of hope would mirror the tenets of womanist theology itself. Womanist theology is inclusive and multigenerational. It resists racism, classism, sexism, heterosexism, ageism, and other oppressions against humanity or nature. A womanist theology of hope denounces the abuse of black women physically or spiritually. It is black women's passion for the possible in this life, undergirded by faith in God's power and Jesus' presence, that has led them across the centuries to fight for voice, humanity, and equality for themselves and their community and that provides the foundation of a prolegomenon for a womanist theology of hope.

---

1. Sonya Sanchez, *Wounded in the House of a Friend* (Boston: Beacon Press), 1995.

Prolegomenon to a Womanist Theology of Hope

Womanist theologians have contributed to the discussion of hope by their references to African American women's hope in their thematic presentations, and in the case of Baker-Fletcher, through her systematic approach to womanist theology. When hope is discussed by womanist theologians, it is a this-worldly empowerment that gains strength from our foremothers and lends transformative possibility for our daughters and sisters in the future. Hope also has sustaining power in the present situations of oppression that bombard African American women from outside as well as from within the African American community. Hope functions as a bridge between oppression and liberation. It was, has been, and is the passion for life's possibilities that led our foremothers—slave, emancipated, and contemporary—to press on in the face of victimization and dehumanizing circumstances. Womanist theologians' work uplifts African American women's embodied passion for life and the possibilities available to African American women empowered by God.

A womanist theology of hope understands African American women's experience as a primary source for the theological task. Their experience includes the historical legacy of the abuse of black women's bodies as well as their ability to survive and overcome oppression. A womanist theology of hope must address the multidimensional oppression of African American women across the generations, from the patriarchal dominant society but also from within the black community and the black church. If womanist theology begins with the experience of black women, how can a womanist theology of hope ignore what black women have said about their experience of hope? The work of womanist theologians is very limited in its exploration of black women's experience of hope, their definition of hope, and how hope functioned in their lives—from their narratives. We must go to the firsthand accounts of black women to get their testaments of hope. While womanist theologians have explored the narratives of slave, emancipated, and contemporary black women, they have not centered on their understanding of a theology of hope that is embedded in the fabric of their narratives. While womanist theologians have not specifically written a theology of hope from the firsthand accounts of African American women, they have employed more than a single-vision analysis of their narratives. They have moved beyond the critique of just sexism (as early feminism) or racism (as early black liberation theology) in their discussion of hope. They have moved beyond discussions that center on ontological blackness to multidimensional understanding of oppression in the lives of African American women.

Womanist theologians Grant, Williams, and Baker-Fletcher continue to debunk the myths that have undergirded the abuse of African American women's bodies. The myths, particularly the Jezebel, Sapphire, and Superwoman myths, are still strongly embedded stereotypical notions of black women in America. Grant alludes to the Sapphire myth that has misconstrued the understanding of what it means to be a womanist. African American women who express their passion for life by refusing to be silenced and getting actively involved in the process of sociopolitical and spiritual change are, Grant notes, "strong black women who have sometime been mislabeled as a domineering castrating matriarch."[2] Williams notes:

> The antebellum tradition of masculinizing black women by means of work has given rise to the idea that black women are not feminine and do not desire to be so. This phenomenon of masculinization of the female slave in the South was also supported by the general attitude of the slave holders that blacks could stand any kind of labor, could not be overworked and were "comparatively insensitive to sufferings that would be unbearable to whites." This meant then, that black women were considered to have far more physical strength and more capacity for pain than white women. The image of black women as superwomen emerged from these kinds of ideas and practices.[3]

Williams seeks to elucidate the emotional and spiritual strength of African American women but also present them as vulnerable, hurting humans who struggle to overcome oppression. Womanist theologians are also critiquing stereotypical depictions of black women in contemporary movies, television, videos, and other media. However, this critique and its discussion have remained primarily within academic circles. The bridge of hope was forged by grassroots women, as well as academics. Grassroots women's critiques in general and of "media and myths and black women" cannot be left out of the discussion, lest we oppress our sisters with yet another "ism"—academic elitism.

The Bible is also a primary source for constructing a womanist theology of hope. The Bible, says Grant, gave content to the God-consciousness of black women. It was God's direct revelatory work through Christ and the Bible that informed and shaped the theological understanding of African American women across the centuries. While womanists support the Bible as a primary source for doing theology, they have more often turned to literature and history

---

2. Jacquelyn Grant, *White Women's Christ and Black Women's Jesus: Feminist Christology and Womanist Response* (Atlanta: Scholars Press, 1989), 205.

3. Delores Williams, *Sisters in the Wilderness: The Challenge of Womanist God-Talk* (Maryknoll, N.Y.: Orbis Books, 1993), 70.

as reflections of black women's experiences. If the Bible gives God-content to black women's experience, as Grant has suggested, womanist theologians must look to the Bible with regularity to discern how biblical persons inform and are reflected in the oppression and transformative liberation of black women. Williams's analysis of Hagar is most helpful here. Her discussion of Hagar exemplifies the hermeneutic of suspicion that African American women bring to the biblical text. Williams names her hermeneutic *identification-ascertainment*. This way of interpreting the text allows African American women to identify with biblical characters and events that reflect their struggles, as well as to ascertain biblical characters or events with whom they do not identify. This mode of inquiry calls for subject, communal, and objective interpretation of Scripture, says Williams.[4] This means, for Williams, that traditional ways of understanding the text must be critiqued for interpretations that foster dehumanizing symbols and support victimization of African American women's bodies. As we noted earlier, one such symbol that must be critiqued for Williams is the meaning and implication of Jesus' beaten, battered body on the cross as a symbol of human salvation and hope.

The symbolism of the cross is a critical issue in our discussion of the limits and contributions of womanist theology and the movement toward the development of a womanist theology of hope, because the cross is pivotal to black women's hope. The *empty* cross, not the cross with Jesus' beaten, battered body upon it, has traditionally been a symbol of hope for black people. The empty cross signifies "that trouble don't last always." It has been an emblem of hope for the black church. To be sure, we must critically examine the meaning and messages of Christian symbols and seek symbols that are not oppressive. At the same time, we must express doctrines that are consistent with the character and presence of God and are liberating to the entire human and natural community. To deny the violence of the cross is to deny the reality of human violence in Jesus' life and ours. Jesus, like so many after him—Martin Luther King Jr., Malcolm X, Fannie Lou Hamer—was persecuted because he risked all to stand for human hope and justice. The cross mandates a theology of hope rather than a theology of sacrifice. A theology of hope is the God-consciousness and God-confidence to risk all to fight against injustice and oppression, even if it means that one may be called upon to give one's life. A theology of hope employs a liberating message of the cross that breaks the cycle of violence in African American women's lives. The message of the cross is not one of resignation to violence or demands for revenge, but is a

---

4. Ibid., 149.

passion for justice. It is an awareness of the Christ presence in one's life that empowers women to seize their personal agency to act against, rather than acquiesce to, victimization and oppression. A theology of hope demands that the society, academy, black community, and church break the cycle of violence and counterviolence by moving toward a new humanity that is self-loving, other-affirming, and community creating.

What, then, are the implications for the black church concerning the symbolism of the cross, the abuse of black women's bodies, and hope? Abuse and violence are painful issues for the church. Statistics indicate that 60 percent of women suffer some form of sexual or physical violence by the age of 18.[5] The statistics for women over 18 are no better. Ntozake Shange's thirty-year-old poem concerning the abuse of women is still true today.

> Every three minutes a woman is beaten
> every five minutes a
> woman is raped/every ten minutes
> a little girl is molested . . .
> Every day
> women's bodies are found
> in alleys and bedrooms/at the top of stairs. . . .[6]

Sexual abuse and violence are a denial of the *Imago Dei* in the victim and the victimizer. Abuse and violence disrupt one's psycho-spiritual-sexual integrity. Victims and victimizers sit in the church every Sunday. Yet, for the most part, the church (including the black church) has been (and is) silent on the issue. This silence has been assumed by some to stem from the acceptance of violence as a norm in the black community, a mythology that is perpetrated by the media and embraced by many non-blacks. The silence in the black church stems in part from racial loyalty and the fear and shame that exposure would prompt.[7] Loyalty and devotion to the black family, the black church, and the black community are enormous barriers to breaking the silence about abuse and violence outside, as well as within, the community. In light of the historic abuse and violence against African American women, a critical question to the church is not only how the church views the cross but how the church views the abused and the abusing. In what way is the church complicit with this abuse through its silence? The church's silence

---

5. See Melba Wilson, *Crossing the Boundary: Black Women Survive Incest* (Seattle: Seal Press, 1993).

6. Ntozake Shange, "With No Immediate Cause," in *Nappy Edges* (New York: St. Martin's Press, 1972).

7. Toinette Eugene, "Swing Low, Sweet Chariot!" in *Violence Against Women and Children: A Christian Theological Sourcebook*, ed. Carol J. Adams and Marie Fortune (New York: Continuum, 1985), 187.

suggests that talking about abuse and violence are greater offenses than the acts themselves!

The teaching and preaching of the church can either be roadblocks or resources for addressing sexual abuse and violence. Scripture and doctrines (such as submission and obedience) can be misused and distorted to suggest that abuse is justified, or they can be used to call us to accountability and responsibility in how we relate to one another as fully human beings created in the image of God. The presence of the resurrected Christ in our lives requires of us transformative visions of our own human potential and possibility in the abundance of life. Thus, the church must exercise a theology of hope that dares to preach and teach against violence and offer safe space, liberative words, support groups, and community resources to the broken and abused.

Womanist theology affirms a theology of hope that liberates African American women, African American men and children, as well as humanity in general, and the cosmos. Womanist theologians must continue their dialogue in the academy and the church and work for new relational paradigms that foster abundant life. We must continue to question, even challenge, oppressive symbols, institutions, and paradigms that deny humanity and empowering life for abused women. While many not-so-new issues, like the abuse of women, continue to "surface" and questions arise, the struggle for responses cannot be devoid of the text, revisited, reconstructed, or reimaged to speak to the experience of the African American woman. Nor can the Christian symbols, such as the cross, be appropriated in ways that contradict the character of God or relieve humanity of its culpability. Breaking the tyranny of silence in the church regarding violence is a multifocal process, but it begins with acknowledging that all humans are created in the image of God and worthy of love. Love of neighbor, self-love, and self-care are primary Christian mandates. They do not permit one to live only in the Holler. Those who love themselves do not beat their neighbor, silently watch their neighbor being beaten, or acquiesce to being beaten. Neighbor love prompts the church to action on behalf of the abused and abusing. Self-care empowers us to remember that Jesus loved "neighbors" enough to suffer abuse and violence on the cross as a witness to humanity that abuse and violence are his crosses to bear, not ours.

The introductory work gleaned from the voices of black women across the centuries and reflected in the works of contemporary womanist theologians coalesce into prolegomenon for a womanist theology of hope. The journey between violence, abuse, and transformation is an arduous one. Traversing the chasm between oppression and transformation is a bridge—womanist hope. Womanist hope is an active hope in the struggle for resurrected transformed existence. It is the embodied hope of African American women that moves the personal, social, and political cogs in the wheels of the transformative process. Embodied hope is a lived witness that discerns God's presence in the experience of African American women. Womanist hope is the bridge constructed with theological belief and social justice that binds and strengthens the community. This bridge of hope welcomes the Hagars, the Sojourners, and the unnamed women. It connects us to every African American woman (man and child) who has suffered abuse and seeks hope. This multigenerational spiritual bridge symbolizes hope that exemplifies our resolute refusal to die as victims, and our undaunted determination to live as vessels of hope. As womanist theology continues to develop as an academic discussion in dialogue with grassroots women, black men, the church, and society, a womanist theology of hope will be birthed from the prolegomena that have been foundational to its life and vitality. I join hands with my sisters, Grant, Williams, Baker-Fletcher, Townes, and Hayes (and others who stand in solidarity against oppression in any form) to construct a womanist bridge, not built on our backs or our bodies, but on our informed engagement of life through the power of the Holy Spirit. There is Hope in the Holler.

Bibliography

Adams, Carol J., and Marie Fortune, eds. *Violence Against Women and Children: A Christian Theological Sourcebook*. New York: Continuum, 1995.

Anderson, Victor. *Beyond Ontological Blackness: An Essay on African American Religious and Critical Criticism*. New York: Continuum, 1995.

Angelou, Maya. *Gather Together in My Name*. New York: Random House, 1974.

―――. *The Heart of a Woman*. New York: Random House, 1981.

―――. *I Know Why the Caged Bird Sings*. New York: Random House, 1970.

―――. *Singin' and Swingin' and Gettin' Merry Like Christmas*. New York: Random House, 1976.

―――. *Wouldn't Take Nothing for My Journey Now*. Hingham, Mass.: Wheeler Publishers, 1994.

Anzaldua, Gloria, and Cherrie Moraga, eds. *The Bridge Called My Back: Writings by Radical Women of Color*. Watertown, Mass.: Persephone Press, 1981.

Baker, T. Lindsay and Julia Baker, eds. *The WPA Oklahoma Slave Narratives*. Norman: University of Oklahoma Press, 1996.

Baker-Fletcher, Karen. *A Singing Something: Womanist Reflections on Anna Julia Cooper*. New York: Crossroad, 1994.

Baker-Fletcher, Karen, and Garth KASIMU Baker-Fletcher. *My Brother, My Sister: Womanist and Xodus God-Talk*. Maryknoll, N.Y.: Orbis Books, 1997.

Barrett, Lindon. "Self-Knowledge, Law, and African American Autobiography: Lucy Delaney's 'From the Darkness Cometh the Light.'" In *The Culture of Autobiography: Construction of Self-Representation*, ed. Robert Folkenflik. Stanford, Calif.: Stanford University Press, 1993.

Berger, Peter. *The Sacred Canopy: Elements of a Sociological Theory of Religion*. Garden City, N.Y.: Doubleday & Co., 1967.

Bloch, Ernst. *A Philosophy of the Future*. New York: Herder and Herder, 1963.

Bogin, Ruth, and Bert James Loewenberg, eds. *Black Women in Nineteenth Century American Life: Their Words, Their Thoughts, Their Feelings*. University Park: Pennsylvania State University Press, 1976.

Bosman, William. *A New and Accurate Description of the Coast of Guinea*. London: Frank Cass, 1967 [1705], 208–11. Quoted in Deborah Gray White, *Ar'n't I a Woman?* 29. New York: W. W. Norton, 1985.

Brim, Clara; quoted in George Rawick, *The American Slave*. Vol. 1. Westport, Conn.: Green-wood Press, 1972.

Bromberg, Pamela S. "The Development of Narrative Technique in Margaret Drabble's Novel." *Journal of Narrative Techniques* 16 (fall 1986): 179.

Burton, Martha Spence; quoted in George Rawick, *The American Slave*. Vol. 4. Westport, Conn.: Greenwood Press, 1972.

Butterfield, Stephen. *Black Autobiography in America*. Amherst: University of Massachusetts Press, 1974.

Canaan, Andrea R. "I Call Up Names: Facing Childhood Sexual Abuse." In *The Black Women's Health Book: Speaking for Ourselves*, ed. Evelyn White, 78–81. Seattle: Seal Press, 1994.

Cannon, Katie Geneva. *Black Womanist Ethics*. Atlanta: Scholars Press, 1988.

———. *Katie's Canon: Womanism and the Soul of the Black Community*. New York: Continuum, 1995.

Carter, Harold. *The Prayer Tradition of Black People*. Valley Forge, Penn.: Judson Press, 1976.

Chapman, G. Clark. "Black Theology and Theology of Hope: What Have They to Say to Each Other?" In *Black Theology: A Documentary History, 1966–1979*, ed. Gayraud S. Willmore and James H. Cone, 193–215. Maryknoll, N.Y.: Orbis Books, 1979.

Coleman, Will. *A Study of African American Slave Narratives as a Source for a Contemporary, Constructive Black Theology*. Ann Arbor, Mich.: University Microfilms International, 1993.

Cone, James, ed. *Black Theology: A Documentary History*. Vol. 1. Maryknoll, N.Y.: Orbis Books, 1979.

———, ed. *Black Theology: A Documentary History*. Vol. 2. Maryknoll, N.Y.: Orbis Books, 1985.

———. *A Black Theology of Liberation: Twentieth Anniversary Edition*. Maryknoll, N.Y.: Orbis Books, 1993.

———. *God of the Oppressed*. New York: Seabury Press, 1988.

Cooper, Anna Julia. *A Voice from the South*. Xenia, Ohio: Aldine Publishing House, 1892; reprint, New York: Oxford University Press, 1988.

Crawford, Vicki L., Jacqueline Anne Rouse, and Barbara Woods, eds. *Women in the Civil Rights Movement: Trailblazers and Torchbearers, 1941–1965*. Bloomington: Indiana University Press, 1993.

Cummings, George. "The Slave Narrative as a Source of Black Theological Discourse: The Spirit and Eschatology." In *Cut Loose Your Stammering Tongue: Black Theology in the Slave Narratives*, ed. Dwight Hopkins and George Cummings, 46–66. Maryknoll, N.Y.: Orbis Books, 1991.

Davis, Charles T., and Henry Louis Gates, eds. *The Slave's Narrative*. New York: Oxford University Press, 1985.

Delaney, Lucy A. *From Darkness Cometh the Light or Struggle for Freedom*. St. Louis: Publishing House of J. T. Smith, 1891; repr. in *Six Women's Slave Narratives*, ed. Henry Louis Gates. New York: Oxford University Press, 1988.

The Diary of Mary Boykin Chestnut, 1861. Quoted in bell hooks, *Ain't I a Woman? Black Women and Feminism*, 53–54. Boston: South End Press, 1981.

Douglass, Frederick. *My Bondage and My Freedom*. New York: Miller, Orton & Mulligan, 1855.

Drumgoold, Kate. "A Slave Girl's Story"; repr. in *Six Women's Slave Narratives*, ed. Henry Louis Gates Jr. New York: Oxford University Press, 1988.

Duster, Alfreda, ed. *Crusade for Justice: The Autobiography of Ida B. Wells*. Chicago: University of Chicago Press, 1970.

Eugene, Toinette M. "A Hermeneutical Challenge for Womanists: The Interrelation Between the Text and Our Experience." In *Perspectives on Feminist Hermeneutics*, ed. Gail Gerber Koontz and Willard Swartley, 20–28. Elkhart, Ind.: Institute of Mennonite Studies, 1986.

————. "'Swing Low, Sweet Chariot!': A Womanist Ethical Response to Sexual Violence and Abuse." In *Violence Against Women and Children· A Christian Theological Sourcebook*, ed. Carol J. Adams and Marie Fortune, 185–200. New York: Continuum, 1995.

Evans, James. *We Have Been Believers: An African American Systematic Theology*. Minneapolis: Fortress Press, 1992.

Folkenflik, Robert, ed. *The Culture of Autobiography: Construction of Self-Representation*. Stanford, Calif.: Stanford University Press, 1993.

Fortune, Marie. *Sexual Violence: The Unmentionable Sin*. Cleveland: Pilgrim Press, 1983.

Frazier, E. Franklin. *The Negro Family in the United States*. Chicago: University of Chicago Press, 1939.

Garrow, David J., ed. *The Montgomery Bus Boycott and the Women Who Started It: The Memoir of Jo Ann Gibson Robinson*. Knoxville: University of Tennessee Press, 1987.

Gates, Henry Louis Jr., ed. *The Classic Slave Narratives*. New York: Penguin Books, 1987.

————. *Narrative of Sojourner Truth: A Bondswoman of Olden Time, with a History of Her Labors and Correspondence from her "Book of Life."* New York: Oxford University Press, 1991.

————. *Six Women's Slave Narratives*. The Schomburg Library of Nineteenth Century Black Women Writers. New York: Oxford University Press, 1988.

Geertz, Clifford. *The Interpretation of Culture*. New York: Basic Books, 1973.

Giddings, Paula. *When and Where I Enter: The Impact of Black Women on Race and Sex in America*. New York: Bantam Books, 1984.

Gladdy, Mary; quoted in George Rawick, *The American Slave*. Supplement, vol. 3. Westport, Conn.: Greenwood Press, 1972.

Goatley, David Emmanuel. *Were You There? Godforsakenness in Slave Religion*. Maryknoll, N.Y.: Orbis Books, 1996.

Goldberg, Michael. *Theology and Narrative: A Critical Introduction*. Philadelphia: Trinity Press International, 1991.

Grant, Jacquelyn. "Black Theology and the Black Woman." In *Black Theology: A Documentary History 1966–1979*, ed. Gayraud S. Wilmore and James H. Cone, 418–33. Maryknoll, N.Y.: Orbis Books, 1979.

————. "Come to My Help, Lord, for I'm in Trouble: Womanist Jesus and the Mutual Struggle for Liberation." In *Reconstructing the Christ Symbol*, ed. M. Stevens. Mahwah, N.J.: Paulist Press, 1994.

————. *Perspectives on Womanist Theology*. Atlanta: ITC Press, 1995.

————. "A Refusal to Be Silenced: Reflections on Sojourner Truth." *Sojourners* 15 (1986): 23–25.

————. "The Sin of Servanthood and the Deliverance of Discipleship." *Other Side* 30 (September/October 1994): 36–40, 47.

————. *White Women's Christ and Black Women's Jesus: Feminist Christology and Womanist Response*. Atlanta: Scholars Press, 1989.

————. "Womanist Theology: Black Women's Experience as a Source for Doing Theology, with Special Reference to Christology." *Journal of the Interdenominational Theological Center* 13 (spring 1986): 195–212.

Green, Phyllis; quoted in George Rawick, *The American Slave*. Supplement 1, vol. 11. Westport, Conn.: Greenwood Press, 1972.

Gusdorf, George. "Conditions and Limits of Autobiography." In *Autobiography: Essays Theoretical and Critical*, ed. James Olney. Princeton, N.J.: Princeton University Press, 1980.

Hardy, Kenneth. *The Pyschological Residuals of Slavery*. Video produced by Stephen Lerner. Topeka, Kan.: Equal Partners Production, 1995.

Hine, Darlene Clark. *Black Women in America: An Historical Encyclopedia*. Brooklyn: Carson Publishing, Inc., 1993.

————. "Rape and the Inner Lives of Black Women in the Middle West." *Signs: Journal of Women in Culture and Society*, vol. 14, no. 4 (1989): 912–20.

Hine, Darlene Clark, Elsa Barkley Brown, and Rosalyn Terbog-Penn. *Black Women in America: An Historical Encyclopedia*. Bloomington: Indiana University Press, 1994.

Hine, Darlene Clark, and Kathleen Thompson, eds. *The Shining Thread of Hope: The History of Black Women in America*. New York: Broadway Books, 1998.

Hollies, Linda. "A Daughter Survives Incest: A Retrospective Analysis." In *The Black Women's Health Book: Speaking for Ourselves*, ed. Evelyn White, 82–91. Seattle: Seal Press, 1994.

Holte, James Craig. *The Ethnic I: A Sourcebook for Ethnic-American Autobiography*. New York: Greenwood House, 1988.

hooks, bell. *Ain't I a Woman? Black Women and Feminism*. Boston: South End Press, 1981.

Hoover, Theresa. "Black Women and the Churches: Triple Jeopardy." In *Black Theology: A Documentary History, 1966–1972*, ed. Gayraud S. Wilmore and James H. Cone, 377–88. Maryknoll, N.Y.: Orbis Books, 1979.

Hopkins, Dwight, ed. *Cut Loose Your Stammering Tongue: Black Theology in the Slave Narratives*. Maryknoll, N.Y.: Orbis Books, 1991.

Hunter, Patricia. "Women's Power—Women's Passion." In *A Troubling in My Soul: Womanist Perspectives on Evil and Suffering*, ed. Emilie M. Townes, 189–98. Maryknoll, N.Y.: Orbis Books, 1993.

Jacobs, Harriet. *Incidents in the Life of a Slave Girl*. Boston: Published by Author, 1861; repr., New York: Oxford University Press, 1988.

Johnson, Clifton. *God Struck Me Dead: Religious Conversion Experiences and Autobiographies of Ex-Slaves*. Philadelphia: Pilgrim Press, 1969.

Johnson, Elizabeth. *She Who Is: The Mystery of God in Feminist Theological Discourse*. New York: Crossroad, 1992.

Jones, Major J. *Black Awareness: A Theology of Hope*. Nashville: Abingdon Press, 1971.

Jones, William R. *Is God a White Racist? A Preamble to Black Theology*. Garden City, N.Y.: Anchor Press, 1978.

————. "Theodicy: The Controlling Category for Black Theology." *Journal of Religious Thought* 30 (1973): 28–38.

Jordan, Winthrop D. *White Over Black American Attitudes Toward the Negro, 1550–1812*. Chapel Hill: University of North Carolina Press, 1968, 150. Quoted in Deborah Gray White, *Ar'n't I a Woman?* 29. New York: W. W. Norton, 1985.

Kierkegaard, Søren. *Christian Discourses*. London: Oxford University Press, 1939.
———. *The Sickness Unto Death: A Christian Psychological Exposition for Upbuilding and Awakening*. Princeton, N.J.: Princeton University Press, 1963.
Lerner, Gerda. *Black Women in White America: A Documentary History*. New York: Vintage Books, 1992.
———. *The Majority Finds Its Past: Placing Women in American History*. New York: Oxford University Press, 1979.
McKay, Nellie Y. "Nineteenth-Century Black Women's Spiritual Autobiographies: Religious Faith and Self Empowerment." In *Interpreting Women's Lives: Feminist Theory and Personal Narratives*, ed. The Personal Narratives Group. Bloomington: Indiana University Press, 1989.
Mellon, James, ed. *Bullwhip Days: The Slave Remembers*. New York: Hastings Weidenfeld and Nicolson, 1988.
The Memoir of Old Elizabeth, a Coloured Woman (1863). Repr. in *Six Women's Slave Narratives*, ed. Henry Louis Gates Jr. The Schomburg Library of Nineteenth Century Black Women Writers. New York: Oxford University Press, 1988.
Mills, Kay. *This Little Light of Mine: The Life of Fannie Lou Hamer*. New York: Penguin Books, 1993.
Moltmann, Jurgen. *Theology of Hope. On the Ground and Implications of a Christian Eschatology*. New York: Harper & Row, 1967.
Moynihan, Daniel Patrick. *The Negro Family, the Case for National Action*. Washington, D.C.: Office of Policy Planning and Research, 1965.
Nickerson, Margaret; quoted in George Rawick, *The American Slave*. Vol. 17. Westport, Conn.: Greenwood Press, 1972.
Olney, James, ed. *Autobiography: Essays Theoretical and Critical*. Princeton, N.J.: Princeton University Press, 1980.
Painter, Nell Irvin. *Sojourner Truth: A Life, a Symbol*. New York: W. W. Norton, 1996.
Personal Narratives Group, ed. *Interpreting Women's Lives: Feminist Theory and Personal Narratives*. Bloomington: Indiana University Press, 1989.
Peterson, Merrill D., ed. *The Portable Thomas Jefferson*. New York: Viking Press, 1974.
Pinn, Anthony B. *Why, Lord? Suffering and Evil in Black Theology*. New York: Continuum, 1995.
Pringle, Thomas, ed. *History of Mary Prince: Related by Herself* (1831). Repr. in *Six Women's Slave Narratives*, ed. Henry Louis Gates Jr. The Schomburg Library of Nineteenth Century Black Women Writers. New York: Oxford University Press, 1988.
Rawick, George P., ed. *The American Slave: A Composite Autobiography*. 18 vols. Westport, Conn.: Greenwood Press, 1972.
———. *The American Slave: A Composite Autobiography*. Supplement, Series I, 12 vols. Westport, Conn.: Greenwood Press, 1977.
Riggs, Marcia Y. *Awake, Arise and Act: A Womanist Call for Black Liberation*. Cleveland: Pilgrim Press, 1994.
Roberts, J. Deotis. *Liberation and Reconciliation: A Black Theology*. Philadelphia: Westminster Press, 1971.
Rosenblatt, Roger. "Black Autobiography: Life as the Death Weapon." In *Autobiography: Essays Theoretical and Critical*, ed. James Olney. Princeton, N.J.: Princeton University Press, 1980.
Ruether, Rosemary R. *Sexism and God-Talk: Toward a Feminist Theology*. Boston: Beacon Press, 1983.

Ruether, Rosemary R., and Rosemary Keller. *In Our Own Voices: Four Centuries of American Women's Religious Writings*. New York: Harper/San Francisco, 1995.

Shange, Ntozake. *For Colored Girls Who Have Considered Suicide When the Rainbow Is Enuf*. New York: Macmillan, 1975.

———. "With No Immediate Cause." In *Nappy Edges*. New York: St. Martin's Press, 1972.

Smith, Jessie Carney. *Epic Lives: One Hundred Black Women Who Made a Difference*. Detroit: Visible Ink Press, 1993.

Smith, Valerie. Introduction to *Incidents in the Life of a Slave Girl*. Boston: Published by Author, 1861; repr., New York: Oxford University Press, 1988.

South Carolina Gazette, 10 July 1736. Quoted in Deborah Gray White, *Ar'n't I a Woman?* 30. New York: W. W. Norton, 1985.

Stanton, Elizabeth Cady, Susan B. Anthony, and Matilda Joslyn Gage, eds. *History of Woman Suffrage*. Vol. 1. New York: Fowler & Wells, 1881; cited in Nell Painter, *Sojourner Truth: A Life, a Symbol*. New York: W. W. Norton, 1996.

Stewart, Maria. *Productions of Maria Stewart* (1835). Repr. in *Spiritual Narratives*, ed. Henry Louis Gates Jr. The Schomburg Library of Nineteenth Century Black Women Writers. New York: Oxford University Press, 1988.

Tate, Claudia, ed. *Black Women Writers at Work*. New York: Continuum 1983.

Harley, Sharon, and Rosalyn Terborg-Penn. *The Afro-American Woman: Struggles and Images*. Port Washington, N.Y.: National University Publishers, 1978.

Thompson, L. S. *The Story of Mattie Jackson: Her Parentage, Experience of Eighteen Years of Slavery, Incidents During the War, Her Escape; A True Story as Given by Mattie* (1866). Repr. in *Six Women's Slave Narratives*, ed. Henry Louis Gates Jr. The Schomburg Library of Nineteenth Century Black Women Writers. New York: Oxford University Press, 1988.

Townes, Emilie M., ed. *A Troubling in My Soul: Womanist Perspectives on Evil and Suffering*. Maryknoll, N.Y.: Orbis Books, 1993.

———. *Womanist Justice, Womanist Hope*. Atlanta: Scholars Press, 1993.

Truth, Sojourner. *The Narrative of Sojourner Truth: A Bondswoman of Olden Times Emancipated by the New York State Legislature in the Early Part of the Present Century, with a History of Her Labors and Correspondence*. The author, 1875. Repr., New York: Arno Press, 1968; Chicago: Johnson Publishing Co., 1970.

———. *Narrative of Sojourner Truth*. With an Introduction by Margaret Washington. New York: Random House, 1993.

Vicchio, Stephen J. *Voice from the Whirlwind: The Problem of Evil and the Modern World*. Westminster, Md.: Christian Classics, 1989.

Walker, Alice. *The Color Purple*. New York: Washington Square Press, 1982.

———. *In Search of Our Mothers' Gardens: Womanist Prose*. San Diego: Harcourt Brace Jovanovich, 1983.

Wallace, Michele. *Black Macho and the Myth of the Superwoman*. London: John Cader Press, 1979.

Watters, Pat, and Reese Cleghorn. *Climbing Jacob's Ladder: The Arrival of Negroes in Southern Politics*. New York: Harcourt, Brace & World, 1967.

West, Cornel. *Restoring Hope: Conversations on the Future of Black America*. Boston: Beacon Press, 1997.

White, Deborah Gray. *Ar'n't I a Woman? Female Slaves in the Plantation South*. New York: W. W. Norton, 1985.

White, Evelyn C., ed. *The Black Women's Health Book: Speaking for Ourselves*. Seattle: Seal Press, 1994.

————. "Love Don't Always Make It Right: Black Women and Domestic Violence." In *The Black Women's Health Book: Speaking for Ourselves*, ed. Evelyn White, 92–97. Seattle: Seal Press, 1994.

Williams, Delores S. "African American Women Develop a New Theological Vision in the Ecumenical Decade: Churches in Solidarity with Women." *The Brown Papers*, vol. I. Boston: Women's Theological Center Press, 1994.

————. "Sin, Nature, and Black Women's Bodies." In *Ecofeminism and the Sacred,* ed. C. Adams. New York: Continuum, 1993.

————. *Sisters in the Wilderness: The Challenge of Womanist God-Talk*. Maryknoll, N.Y.: Orbis Books, 1993.

————. "Visions, Inner Voices, Apparitions, and Defiance in Nineteenth-Century Black Women's Narratives." *Women's Studies Quarterly* 21 (spring/summer 1993): 81–89.

————. "A Womanist Perspective on Sin." In *A Troubling in My Soul: Womanist Perspectives on Evil and Suffering*, ed. Emilie Townes. Maryknoll, N.Y.: Orbis Books, 1993.

————. "Women's Oppression and Lifelong Politics in Black Women's Religious Narratives." *Journal of Feminist Studies in Religion* 1 (fall 1985): 59–71.

Williams, Frances Barrier. "The Club Movement Among Colored Women in America." In *A New Negro for a New Century*, ed. Booker T. Washington, N. B. Wood, and Fannier Barrier Williams. New York: Arno Press, 1969.

Williams, Juan, ed. *Eyes on the Prize: The American Civil Rights Years, 1954–1965*. New York: Viking Press, 1987.

Wilmore, Gayraud S., and James H. Cone, eds. *Black Theology: A Documentary History, 1966–1979*. Maryknoll, N.Y.: Orbis Books, 1979.

Wilson, Emily Herring. *Hope and Dignity: Older Black Women of the South*. Philadelphia: Temple University Press, 1983.

Wilson, Melba. *Crossing the Boundary: Black Women Survive Incest*. Seattle: Seal Press, 1993.

Woods, Frances. "Take My Yoke Upon You." In *A Troubling in My Soul: Womanist Perspectives on Evil and Suffering*, ed. Emilie M. Townes, 39–41. Maryknoll, N.Y.: Orbis Books, 1993.

Woodward, C. Van. "History from Slave Sources." In *The Slave's Narrative*, ed. Charles T. Davis and Henry Louis Gates Jr. New York: Oxford University Press, 1985.

Yellin, Jean Fagan. "Text and Context of Harriet Jacobs' *Incidents in the Life of a Slave Girl: Written By Herself.*" In *The Slave's Narrative*, ed. Charles T. Davis and Henry Louis Gates Jr., 262–282. New York: Oxford University Press, 1985.

Young, Perry Deane. "A Surfeit of Survey." *Washington Post*, 30 May 1976, B1; cited in Kay Mills, *This Little Light of Mine: The Life of Fannie Lou Hamer*. New York: Penguin Books, 1993.

Index